Swahili beyond the Boundaries

This series of publications on Africa, Latin America, Southeast Asia, and Global and Comparative Studies is designed to present significant research, translation, and opinion to area specialists and to a wide community of persons interested in world affairs. The editor seeks manuscripts of quality on any subject and can usually make a decision regarding publication within three months of receipt of the original work. Production methods generally permit a work to appear within one year of acceptance. The editor works closely with authors to produce a high-quality book. The series appears in a paperback format and is distributed worldwide. For more information, contact the executive editor at Ohio University Press, 19 Circle Drive, The Ridges, Athens, Ohio 45701.

Executive editor: Gillian Berchowitz
AREA CONSULTANTS
Africa: Diane M. Ciekawy
Latin America: Thomas Walker
Southeast Asia: William H. Frederick

The Ohio University Research in International Studies series is published for the Center for International Studies by Ohio University Press. The views expressed in individual volumes are those of the authors and should not be considered to represent the policies or beliefs of the Center for International Studies, Ohio University Press, or Ohio University.

Swahili beyond the Boundaries

LITERATURE, LANGUAGE, AND IDENTITY

Alamin Mazrui

Ohio University Research in International Studies
Africa Series No. 85
Ohio University Press
Athens

© 2007 by the
Center for International Studies
Ohio University
www.ohio.edu/oupress

Printed in the United States of America
All rights reserved

16 15 14 13 12 11 10 09 08 07   5 4 3 2 1

The books in the Ohio University Research in International Studies Series
are printed on acid-free paper ∞ ™

Library of Congress Cataloging-in-Publication Data

Mazrui, Alamin M.
  Swahili beyond the boundaries : literature, language, and identity / Alamin
Mazrui.
    p. cm. — (Ohio University research in international studies. Africa series ;
no. 85)
  Includes bibliographical references and index.
  ISBN-13: 978-0-89680-252-0 (pbk. : alk. paper)
  ISBN-10: 0-89680-252-3 (pbk. : alk. paper)
  1. Swahili literature—History and criticism. 2. Literature and society—
Africa, East. I. Title.
  PL8703.5.b M25 2007
  896.392—dc22

                                                        2006036626

To my wife,

Ousseina Alidou,

and my daughters,

Nuwayla and Salma:

With love and appreciation

for the courage to cross the boundaries

Contents

Acknowledgments

Many of the chapters in this volume are extensive revisions of essays that have been published previously in scholarly journals and edited books. An earlier version of chapter 1 first appeared as "The Swahili Literary Tradition: An Intercultural Heritage" in *The Cambridge History of African and Caribbean Literature*, volume 1, edited by Abiola Irele and Simon Gikandi (Cambridge University Press). The chapter has been updated to include a discussion of numerous literary and other relevant texts that have been published since 2000. Chapter 2 is an extension of thoughts and ideas that go back to my collection of Swahili poetry, *Chembe cha Moyo* (Heinemann, 1988). The linguistic dimension of these ideas came to constitute the body of my article entitled "Conservationism and Liberalism in Swahili Poetry: The Linguistic Dimension" (*Research in African Literatures* 23, no. 4 [1992]: 67–77). Since then, many poetic anthologies have been released, new scholarly contributions have been made to the debate, and, more important, new dynamics in the socioeconomic, political, and media landscape of the Swahili-speaking region have emerged that have had a direct bearing on my analysis.

The part of chapter 4 that focuses on the Swahili translation of Shakespeare's works was the subject of my "Shakespeare in Africa: Between English and Swahili Literature" that appeared in *Research in African Literatures* (27, no. 1 [1996]: 64–79). Here I have included a new perspective from more current readings in translation theories as well as an extensive exploration of the textual and contextual attributes of the Swahili translation of George Orwell's *Animal Farm* as it relates to the politics of post-colonial East Africa. The part on Orwell was first presented at Columbia University in 2001 at the invitation of that institution's Institute of African Studies. I am grateful to the colleagues present in the audience for their comments and feedback. In sum, by revising these essays and assembling them and other relevant material in a single book, I hope to bring the complex issues of Swahili literary identity and its reconfiguration over space and time into sharper relief.

Finally, I would like to thank the College of Humanities at the Ohio State University for granting me a Special Research Assignment quarter—essentially a quarter without teaching responsibilities—during the 2002–3 academic year to travel to East Africa for follow-up fieldwork on this book project. That release time was instrumental in giving the project a new momentum toward its completion.

Introduction

Hybridity Reconfigured

In its liberal as well as conservative definitions, Swahili literature was "traditionally" a complex hybrid space from the earliest years of its formation. The term hybridity is commonly used to refer to "the creation of new transcultural forms within the contact zone produced by colonisation" (Ashcroft, Griffiths, and Tiffin 2003, 118). But the Swahili experience demonstrates that hybridity is a configuration that is not at all new to the human condition. It has existed in many guises in previous historical moments. If its relevance has become more salient in recent years, it is only because of the realization that it has the potential to counter certain historical claims of identitarian politics, especially of the colonial kind.

Because of the colonial fixation with simple binaries and the place of naturalized myths of racial and ethnic origins in imperial ideology, however, the fact of hybridity was often held against the Swahili people[1] and their culture. It was not uncommon in colonialist discourse to find the Swahili described as a "mongrel" people of African and Arab descent and statements that in its disposition this "mutation" encapsulated not the best but the worst of the racially determined cultural attributes of its dual parentage.[2] Yet as Robert Young points out:

1

This naming of human mixture as "degeneracy" both asserts the norm and subverts it, undoing its terms of distinction, and opening up the prospect of the evanescence of "race" as such. Here, therefore, at the heart of racial theory, in its most sinister, offensive move, hybridity also maps out its most anxious, vulnerable site: a fulcrum at its edge and centre where its dialectics of injustice, hatred and oppression can find themselves effaced and expunged. (1995, 19)

In its potential to subvert the colonial norm, hybridity is seen to challenge the validity and authenticity of any essentialist cultural identity. Hybridity is thus positioned as an antithesis to essentialism or "the belief in invariable and fixed properties which define the 'whatness' of a given entity" (Fuss 1991, xi). As the interweaving of elements of the colonizer and the colonized, the hybrid formation provides a representation of cultural difference that is located in between the colonizer and the colonized, constituting a form of "third space" that blurs the limitations of existing boundaries and calling into question established cultural and identitarian categorizations (Bhabha 1994). What I attempt to show in this book is that while hybridity, in its interrogation of fixity and essentialist designations, may indeed evoke endless openness on questions of home and identity, it can simultaneously put closure on specific forms of subjectivity. In recent years, one definition of Swahili literature after another, for example, has accepted Swahiliness in its transethnic hybrid articulation but not in the ethnic sense that native speakers of the language continue to cling to. Let us look at a few examples.[3]

One such transethnic definition is provided by Rainer Arnold, who contends that today Swahili literature "represents no more the Swahili culture and society of the coast only. But it is part and parcel of the society and cultures of the new nations of East Africa. From the scientific point of view it would be more effective to label this literature as East African literature in the Swahili language" (1972, 69). The forces of linguistic expansion and political "modernization"—in the nation-states (Kenya, Uganda, and Tanzania) that have adopted Swahili as their national language—are deemed to have conspired in a way that makes an ethnic definition of Swahili literature somewhat superfluous or even obsolete, in spite of the fact that the depth and degree of Swahilization have varied immensely from nation to nation and from one part of a country to another.

It is possible, of course, to reject the existence of Swahili ethnicity without rejecting the idea of a peculiarly Swahili identity. In Tanzania, for example, quasi-socialist policies that began in the late 1960s resulted in the tendency to generalize Swahili identity beyond the frontiers of Swahili ethnicity. At least in what used to be Tanganyika the term came to refer to virtually any person of African origin within the space of Tanzania. Swahili came to be raised to the level of national identity as a sense of Swahili political culture was evolving. For some, then, Swahili literature increasingly came to designate the literature composed by Africans who had been shaped by this new politico-cultural dispensation. In the words of Kiango and Sengo, for example:

> Kwa hapa kwetu, Kiswahili ndiye mlezi, ametukuza tangu siku za ukoloni na kutuunga pamoja hadi kufika siku za uhuru wetu. Ni lugha inayoeleza utaratibu wetu wa maisha. . . . Mswahili ni Mtanzania na hapana shaka lugha ya Kiswahili ni lugha ya Watanzania. Hivyo, inatazamiwa kwamba watu watakubali kuitwa Waswahili na kujaribu kujenga utamaduni, mila na desturi badala ya kuthamini zaidi ukabila. Na hapo ndipo tutaweza kusema kwamba tunayo fasihi ya Kiswahili. (1972, 10)

> Here at home, Swahili is our guardian; it has nurtured us from the colonial era and united us to the period of independence. It is the language that expresses our social dynamics. . . . A Swahili person means a Tanzanian and there is no doubt that Swahili is the language of Tanzania. Therefore, it is anticipated that people will accept being called Swahili and try to build values, customs and norms [around a transethnic Swahiliness] instead of placing greater value on ethnicity. And that is when we can say that we have a Swahili literature. (My translation)

The politicization of Swahili identity and its equation with the colonial creation called the nation-state is a phenomenon that is peculiarly Tanzanian. Even though Swahili is also the national language of Kenya, the idea that a Kenyan is by definition a Swahili would be alien indeed to the relational universe of the citizens of Kenya, at least for the foreseeable future. But this has not always been true in Tanzania, where ethnicities were subsumed under a national ethos with Swahili as its binding force. It is in this connection that Lodhi, essentially in agreement with Kiango and Sengo, sees the Swahili language as an indispensable catalyst for the Tanzanian syncretism that has resulted in a national culture: "The Tanzania culture . . . is the sum total of all the good customs and traditions of the different language groups in Tanzania. All these regional cultures using local languages, or dialects, are now being transformed into a National Culture using Swahili which is increasingly commanding the loyalty, affection and respect of Tanzanians" (1974, 11). The strong Swahili linguistic nationalism[4] of Tanzania in the immediate aftermath of independence, rooted in the belief in ethnocultural blending, therefore, posed the challenge of reconstructing Swahili literary identity along national boundaries.

Senkoro, still inspired by the Tanzanian concept of Swahili identity, proposes a definition of Swahili literature that transcends the nation-state.

Mwanzoni tulitaja uhusiano wa fasihi na utamaduni wa jamii inayohusika. Uhusiano huu utatusaidia hapa katika kueleza ushairi wa Kiswahili. Tutaamua kuwa kazi fulani ni fasihi ya Kiswahili au la kutokana na jinsi ilivyojitambulisha na ilivyojihusisha na utamaduni wa Kiswahili. Hapa neno Waswahili halimaanishi kabila la Waswahili kwani kabila la namna hiyo halipo leo. Waswahili hapa ni wananchi wa Afrika ya mashariki na kati kwa jumla na wala si wale tu wanaoishi katika pwani ya nchi hizi. (1988, 11)

At the beginning we talked about the relationship between the literature and the culture of the related society. This relationship will help us in defining Swahili poetry. We shall decide that a particular work is or is not Swahili literature on the basis of its association and relationship with the culture of the Swahili people. Here the term "Swahili people" does not mean a Swahili ethnic group, for such an ethnic group does not exist today. The Swahili people here are citizens of East and Central Africa in general and not only those who live on the coastline of these countries. (My translation)

Senkoro thus posits a transnational Swahili culture whose literature, if it is composed in the Swahili language and reflects that Swahili culture, would appropriately be defined as Swahili literature. Swahiliness is seen as a hybrid abstract that transcends both ethnic and national boundaries.

Like Senkoro but without any cultural inferences, Robert Philipson argues for a supranational Swahili literature that would include any literary works in the Swahili language by writers from Kenya, Uganda, and Tanzania and would not necessarily be restricted in scope to writers who are ethnically Swahili or to themes circumscribed by the Swahili cultural experience. This supranational literature, according to Philipson, should also take into account the participation and contribution of the Swahili-speaking communities of Zaire (1990, 2).[5]

All these definitions of Swahili literature demonstrate how one form of hybridity (an ethnically based hybridity long associated with the speakers of Swahili as a native language) is being challenged by a hybridity of another, arguably more dominant, culture of the nation-state or political region. They all privilege the notion that the literature of the twentieth century and beyond is heterogeneous ethnically, nationally, and religiously as well as ideologically. It is sometimes transethnic and transnational, bound by the instrumental force of the Swahili language that, though differentiated,[6] tends to revolve around an evolving standard norm. Swahili as well as non-Swahili, Tanzanian as well as non-Tanzanian, Muslim as well as non-Muslim authors have been participating in and contributing to the creation of this new hybrid literature whose development is explored more fully in chapter 1.

But Swahili literature by no means begins with the inception of European colonial rule in the region. It stretches back for centuries before that. Its language of composition is indeed Swahili, but even more specifically, the variety drawn from its primary dialects that predate the birth of Standard Swahili. It is both oral and written, but the written included the *ajami* tradition, a localized version of the Arabic script. Its themes are mainly, though by no means exclusively, culturally bound to Swahili ethnicity. It is a literature that has a certain history of continuity and fusion with the Arab-Islamic world that continues to influence and shape its modern composers. And this (imagined) hybridity of old is at the root of the literary consciousness of the Swahili people, adding a literary dimension to their sense of shared identity. This identitarian attachment to the "old" is most clearly articulated in the terrain of the linguistics and prosodics of Swahili poetry covered in chapter 2.

Equally important in understanding the reconfiguration of hybridity in the Swahili experience is that certain expressions of hybridity can be more acceptable to some interest groups while other expressions become more acceptable to other groups. I argue in chapter 2 that the politics of poetry and prosodics in Swahili literature is at some level an ideological contestation between two types of elite, each advocating for a kind of literary subjectivity rooted in a particular configuration of literary hybridity. While in their discourse both deny the fact of hybridity in their poetic practice for reasons that are apparently nationalistic, in reality they are drawn to two different (attempted) delineations of hybridity in the space of prosody, one posturing toward the East and the other toward the West.

Contrary to the postcolonial position that hybridity necessarily negates particularity in the domain of identity, chapter 3 demonstrates that certain forms of hybridity can be invoked precisely to affirm subjectivity. Because precolonial Swahili literature—which was already hybrid in its constitution—was more clearly coincident with the Swahili people's particular ethnicity, it has come to assume a special place in their ethnic consciousness. Yet in the study of Swahili literature it is precisely this pre-twentieth-century tradition of Swahili literature that has been subjected to misrepresentations, opening the door for future contestations of the essence of Swahili literary identity. Some of these representations have resulted from an Arab-Islamic bias and others from a modal bias of Eurocentric scholarship, confounding the expression of a Swahili literary identity. Leading Muslim clerics would later argue against "excessive" western influence in Swahili language and literature, depicting such a development as a path toward the de-Swahilization of Swahili verbal culture. Yet, ironically, they proceeded to anchor the "purity" of the Swahili literary tradition in the convergent space of its "admixture" with the expressive traditions of the Arab-Islamic world. The fact of a specific hybrid formation, in other words, becomes the sine qua non of ethnic identity and the basis of attempted closure of the space to other articulations of hybridity.

In addition to the contested location of texts originally composed in Swahili, the (re)configuration of the hybridity characterizing Swahili literature has more recently been compounded by a new factor: works translated into Swahili from other linguistic sources. East Africa has a long tradition of works translated into Swahili from other cultures. In postcolonial East Africa some of these translated works were inscribed in academic curricula not as texts of a foreign literature in Swahili but as part of the corpus of texts of Swahili literature.

It is possible that a certain paucity of Swahili literary texts in print in the newly evolved genres of the novel and play—the Swahili written poetic tradition, which is rich, spans several centuries—initially triggered the rehabilitation of translated texts and their subsequent incorporation into the Swahili literary organism. What may have started as a response to some ad hoc need, however, soon came to have a legitimacy of its own, shaking the boundaries between literature in (Swahili) translation and literature in the Swahili original. Increasingly, some writers (e.g., Kazungu 1984;

Mazrui 1981b; Ryanga 1985; Ntarangwi 2004) began to include translated texts in their definition of Swahili literature.

In 1995, there was a newspaper debate on the scope of literary studies in Kenya in which the noted literary critic Chris Wanjala drew a comparison between English literature and Swahili literature as taught in the country's institutions of higher learning. In his typically provocative style, Wanjala claimed that in contrast to its English counterpart, the Swahili-literature syllabus was rather narrow, focusing on East African writers to the exclusion of artists from other parts of the world: "Although there are so many students who study Swahili in secondary schools and universities, teachers of Swahili pick adequate theories of linguistics at the expense of adequate texts of study in the world context. They operate on a narrow skeleton of literary texts and only from the East African region" (1995, 12). In spite of the fact that literary texts in Swahili original are produced primarily by writers from East Africa—although literary productions are beginning to emerge in the Swahili Diaspora—Wanjala considers the focus on texts from this region for Swahili-literature courses to be unduly insular.

To remedy this situation, Wanjala recommends that Swahili literature "include studies in Indian, American, European literatures" as well as literatures from North Africa and the Middle East, presumably in Swahili translation. Yet in the rest of his article, Wanjala clearly regards original composition in the English language as essential to his conception of literature in English. He also regards Japanese, Soviet, Polish, and "other" literatures in English translation as appropriate not for courses in English literature but for those in comparative literature. But he does not find it anomalous that the study of Swahili literature should include "other" literatures in Swahili translation (1995, 68).

Wanjala's critics were quick to question his facts but not his terms of reference about the state of Swahili literary studies in Kenya. Sheri Mwimali, for example, noted that contrary to Wanjala's presumption, university students of Swahili literature were already being exposed to a wide range of translated texts from other countries, mentioning translated works of Sophocles,

Shakespeare, Orwell, Gogol, Ayi Kwei Armah, Ferdinand Oyono, Robert Serumaga, Chinua Achebe, and Wole Soyinka (1995, 19). Likewise, Mwenda Mbatiah claimed that at the University of Nairobi, they had all along been "teaching translated works from all parts of the world" in Swahili-literature courses. Mbatiah asked: "So where does Wanjala get the idea that the Swahili literature syllabus is narrow?" (1995, 19).

Perhaps not all translated texts get domesticated to the extent of incorporation into Swahili-literature courses. In spite of Ryanga's assessment that European translators of English texts into Swahili were more competent translators than their more recent African counterparts (1985, 170), for example, none of the texts rendered into Swahili by the former has ever been adopted into Swahili-literature courses. Does the identity of the translator matter at all? Or is it the message that is at stake? And how about considerations of form? There may indeed be several reasons that explain why some translated texts get assimilated into Swahili literature and others do not.

Edward Fitzgerald's version of the *Rubaiyat of Omar Khayyam* is now considered part of literature in English. But it can be argued that Fitzgerald breathed his own literary genius into an independent interpretation of the worldview of the Persian poet of the twelfth century. There is even debate as to whether Fitzgerald's work was an exercise in translation at all or whether the man merely drew inspiration from Khayyam's verses to craft an entirely independent masterpiece (Dashti 1971, 167). Agreeing with the latter position, Ali Mazrui argues that only Swahili reinterpretations of "foreign" texts of Fitzgeraldian proportion could justifiably be added to the corpus of literature in Swahili (1995b, 14). Whatever the case, the place and role of translated works constitutes another important dimension in the (re)configuration of Swahili literature, the subject matter of chapter 4, adding a new face to its hybrid constitution.

In sum, then, the term "Swahili literature" has come to have multiple and expanding meanings of hybridity, complicated not only by questions of literary history and interpretation, by contestations about literary form and style (especially in poetry), but also by the possibilities of migration of texts from one universe of culture to another.

The nature of the issues discussed above point to the importance of studying the literatures of the "other." Various reasons can be advanced for studying the literatures of other societies. One is the quest for an aesthetic and literary experience that is cross cultural. Another reason is to gain a better understanding of those other societies. In the words of Henry James, "It takes a great deal of history to produce a little literature." Sometimes a command of the best literature of another society may be a better guide to that society than many history books about it. Yet another reason for studying "foreign" literature is to understand one's own society better. According to the great Swahili poet Shaaban Robert (1909–62), *"Fasihi kioo cha Mngu"* (Literature Is the Mirror of God). We look at the creative mind in other societies in the hope that we will begin to understand our own society better. Comparative literature can indeed be a mirror to our culture.

But there are more specific reasons why this comparative agenda in the western academy must include Africa. The first reason has to do with the kind of literary legacy African literature bears in relation to language. If the African continent is the cradle of the human species, it is also the birthplace of human languages. Quite remarkably, the consequences of that simple observation have continued to the present day. Africa has a bigger range of languages than any other continent in the world. With only an eighth of the population of the world, Africa has nearly a third of its languages, depending on where one draws the line between language and dialect.

The diversity of African languages is also impressive. There are tonal and nontotal, click and nonclick, genderized and neutered languages, local tongues and transcontinental families such as the Afro-Asiatic and Semitic clusters. This immense inheritance has continued to provide linguists with innumerable challenges and opportunities in the testing and (re)construction of linguistic theories.

Africa's wealth in languages, however, has only just begun to be tapped internationally for what it has to offer in literary terms. There are African languages which have had written literatures for centuries, such as Amharic, Hausa, and Swahili. Then there are a wider variety of African languages that, until recently, had been transmitting their literary jewels exclusively by word of mouth across generations, such as Somali, Yoruba, and Zulu languages.

The world of western scholarship was introduced to the written traditions of African literatures late in the nineteenth century, but the West has been struggling with Africa's immense oral tradition only since the second half of the twentieth century. The retrieval process has been gathering momentum, but there are still fields and fields of unexplored territory.

In the history of western literature there were times when a person could be brilliant with the pen but banal and mediocre in conversation. Such was said of Oliver Goldsmith, the seventeenth-century poet and novelist. In many African societies that have only recently embraced writing, however, the reverse was often the case. A person could be nervous when holding a pen but truly eloquent in the free flow of oral creativity. There is a school of thought in English literature that poetry should approximate the ordinary language of conversation, but with the emphasis on the oral, many in Africa would argue that it is ordinary conversation that should try to approximate the elegant language of poetry. And ultimately, the centrality of oral literature in these societies accorded special status to Africa's griots and bards, who acted not only as poets but played roles that in industrialized societies are the preserve of historians, journalists, political commentators, preachers, and moral philosophers.

The continuing legacy of orality in much of the literature in African languages has had an impact on the world literary scene in very significant ways. Most fundamentally, it has upset received ideas about the very definition of "literature," a term that implied writing. Furthermore, the domain of orality has had a profound influence on Africa's written literature, stimulating the evolution of new forms of realism. As the rhythms and patterns of orality continue to be recreated by African novelists, these new realisms are beginning to challenge the "canon" in world literature in general and literature in English in particular toward greater "multiculturalization." In the process, Africa's literary experiences are inscribing themselves in new ways in literary theoretical discourses that had long been based primarily on the reading of western texts.

Another major reason for paying attention to literature in African languages concerns the African continent itself, where three and sometimes four widely divergent civilizations—African, Indian, Arab-Islamic, and western—converge. Of course, neither multiculturalism nor multilingualism is unique to Africa. Emperor Charles of the Holy Roman Empire is reported to have said, "To God I speak Spanish, to women Italian, to men French, and to my horse—German." It is also true that the English language has absorbed a lot of vocabulary from divergent sources. But both the multilingualism of European royalty and the absorptive range of English have been confined primarily to European languages.

What is linguistically ecumenical about Africa is that it has drawn from a much wider cultural spectrum. Some of its languages have assimilated over a third of their vocabulary from civilizations outside Africa. Even when we are studying literature in African indigenous languages, therefore, we are often studying cultural hybridity at work. Literature in languages such as Hausa, Swahili, and Wolof had for centuries been a conversation between Africanity and Islam—from North Africa through Arabia to Persia. The influence of western India, especially on Swahili society, goes back to the thirteenth century, first on its material culture and much later on its popular song and musical culture. The twentieth century added Islam, Asian infusions, and the impact of the West on indigenous cultures, modifying the cultural synthesis of preceding generations. Studying African literatures across time would clearly manifest these layers of the cultural geology and dynamics of Africa's artistic hybridity.

In sum, then, this book is not intended to be merely a contribution to the understanding of Swahili literature and its recent development in the direction of new forms of hybridization. It is also an exercise in comparative literature, with the objective of promoting a more multicultural understanding of literature as a human experience.

Finally, a word about terminology. As Mazrui and Shariff argued in their book *The Swahili: Idiom and Identity* (1994), writing about a particular people in a language that is foreign to them poses a problem of choice between a terminology of authenticity and a terminology of intelligibility. With regard to Swahili studies, in particular, the tradition of terminological authenticity has sought to maintain a distinction between the following derivatives as used by Swahili-speaking people:

Kiswahili	=	Swahili language
Mswahili	=	Swahili person
Waswahili	=	Swahili people
Uswahili	=	Swahili culture and ways of life
Uswahilini	=	land of the Swahili-speaking people

The tradition of terminological intelligibility, on the other hand, shows greater sensitivity to the linguistic rules of the medium of discourse, in this case the English language. The English-speaking people refer to their language as "English," but in Swahili, forced to conform to structural rules of the Bantu language, it is known as "Kiingereza." Similarly, the French refer to their French language as "français." Intelligibility will likely suffer if we retain the French term in an English sentence: "Français is found in over twenty African nations."

The same logic applies to Swahili. Observing the different derivations of the term "Swahili" would be in accord with the morphological rules of the Swahili language but not of English—the medium used in this book. To do so would be to maintain authenticity at the expense of intelligibility.

Many African nationalists are strong advocates of terminological authenticity and may consider a departure from this tradition as a kind of terminological "betrayal." But because readers may include those who are not familiar with the Swahili language, I have opted to not follow the common Swahili nationalist terminological practice in the interest of terminological intelligibility. Throughout this text, therefore, "Swahili" will appear independently without the usual affixes that distinguish between the language, the culture, the people, and their homeland.

1

The Intercultural Heritage
of Swahili Literature

Swahili literature, broadly defined as that body of verbal art originally composed in the Swahili language, has been a hybrid formation for several centuries. It is a product of what Ali Mazrui has
termed Africa's triple heritage, emerging out of a confluence of
three forces: the indigenous tradition, the Islamic legacy, and the
western impact. The indigenous contribution has, of course, fea-
tured primarily in the realm of orature, but over the years it has
continued to affect the destiny of Swahili written literature that
is the focus of this chapter. One must also bear in mind that the
boundary of what is written and what is oral in the various genres
of Swahili literature is not always easy to determine.

Until relatively recently, the general tendency among scholars
with regard to the interaction between the Arab-Islamic and indigenous factors was to privilege the former (usually seen as the
"donor") over the latter (regarded as the "recipient"), to a point
where it has supposedly lost its local identity. But as Ohly observes, "The overlapping of these two cultures—the local, Bantu
and the Oriental—took place on the basis of mutual adjustment
and not, as has been thought until now, on the basis of assimilation,
so that a two-tiered development of literature can be observed
which embraces both the pure elements of Bantu folk culture and

the inflowing Muslim-Oriental elements" (1985, 461). In fact, the so-called layers became integrated into a new organic synthesis that in time fused with other influences and reflects, among other things, the tensions between town and country, between "gentry" and "commoner," and "the contradictory consciousness of the Swahili crowd" (Glassman 1995, 1–25).

The beginnings of writing in Swahili literature can be traced to the Afro-Arab contact on the East African seaboard that goes back to antiquity. According to the accounts of *The Periplus of the Erythrean Sea* (by an unknown Greek author), Arab and Persian traders must have frequented the East African coast as early as the first century AD, if not earlier. Recurrent waves of Arabian migrants were displaced by internecine wars in their own countries and found refuge and eventually settled in the East African city-states. Over time, many of these settlers intermarried with the local population, and Islam, which established itself in the area soon after it was founded in Arabia, became an additional force in the consolidation of this Afro-Arab heritage. It is out of this cultural intercourse that the Swahili written tradition was initially born.

This first wave of writing used Swahilized versions of the Arabic alphabet akin to what is referred to as *ajami* in West Africa.[1] Exactly when this mode of writing came into being in the Swahili literary tradition is difficult to determine. The *Hamziyya* poem celebrating the life of Prophet Muhammad, for example, is said to have been composed no later than AD 1652 (Knappert 1979, 103). The earliest surviving Swahili manuscript, however, which is dated about AD 1728, is Mwengo wa Athumani's *Utenzi wa Herekali* (The Epic of Herakleios)—also known as *Chuo cha Tambuka* (The Book of Tabuk)—on the seventh-century encounter between the troops of the Byzantine emperor Herakleois and those of the Prophet Muhammad (Gerard 1981, 96).

This pre-twentieth-century literature was replete with homiletic *tenzi* or *tendi* (sing. *utenzi* and *utendi*, respectively), verses with a didactic or hagiographic thrust. The term *utenzi* generally refers to an extended narrative poem of defined meter and rhyme that often assumes an epical form and function. Structurally, the *utenzi* verse is made up of four lines—or, in the opinion of some, two with a caesura—with eight syllables to a line and an aaab rhyming pattern. Its language is often simple, making little use of such features as extended metaphors, allegories, and symbolism. And because of its structural and stylistic simplicity, it has lent itself well to lengthy versification of historical events and fictional narratives. There are *tenzi* on legendary characters such as Fumo Liyongo, on the lives of various prophets of Islam, on wars and battles within Swahililand and elsewhere, and on many other subjects requiring extensive articulation. The *utenzi* can run into thousands of verses. Shaaban Robert's *Utenzi wa Vita vya Uhuru* (1967a), an account of World War II from a Tanzanian perspective, for example, is comprised of some three thousand verses.

The celebrated *tenzi* of this period of the early eighteenth century include Sayyid Abdalla bin Ali bin Nasir's *Takhmisa ya Liyongo* (on the events surrounding the life and tragic end of the Swahili poet-hero, Fumo Liyongo); Abdalla Mas'ud Mazrui's *Utenzi wa Al-Akida* (a historical chronicle in verse of the intrigues in the power struggles between the *akida* [commander] Muhammad bin Mbarak Mazrui and the Omani governor of Mombasa); and Abubakar Mwengo's *Utenzi wa Katirifu* (on the supposed romance between a wealthy Muslim man and Hasina, the daughter of a slain "pagan" king, that leads to conspiracies and a series of battles between Muslim forces and those of nonbelievers in Islam).

It is also from this period that we have records of the celebrated woman poet Mwana Kupona binti Mshamu (AD 1810–60) and her poem *Utendi wa Mwana Kupona*. Composed in 1858 shortly before her death, the poem was intended to be an instructional guide for her seventeen-year-old daughter, Mwana Hashima binti Mataka, on the place, roles, duties, and responsibilities of a woman with respect to her husband. Today, the work stands as one of the most famous among the *tenzi*. Its accomplishments can be attributed as much to its tone and humor as to the flow of its language and the style intrinsic to the work. "The poem is a masterpiece of allusions that play up the male ego in a society where men see themselves as masters over their womenfolk, while at the same time instructing the intelligent woman to treat the opposite sex as she would an infant" (Shariff 1991b, 46). More recently, in fact, the poem has begun to generate some controversy as to its ideological orientation. Some argue that it affirms and reinforces the patriarchal order in Swahili society, while others see in it a subversive, if disguised, antihegemonic discourse. Amid this controversy, however, Mwana Kupona continues to enjoy a place of note among Swahili poets: shops, restaurants, sewing businesses, and cultural forums are some of the projects that bear her name.

While Mwana Kupona has rightly attracted the greatest attention among women poets, women have generally had a profound influence on Swahili verse. Even when women do not receive the acclaim that they deserve, some of the best verse in the Swahili literary tradition continues to be the products of women's genius. Furthermore, women have been central in the conservation of works of poetry of the classical type, both in their oral and written forms, and it is to them that people usually turn for the most eloquent recitations. Ali A. Jahadhmy has noted, in connection with the Swahili of the island of Lamu, that women "in the past as well as in the present have been the custodians of Swahili poetry; in fact, some of the best verse literature has come from the pen of women. . . . Zena Mahmud has just completed a most authoritative work on Swahili poetry. . . . She is, with a few others, carrying on the tradition of the women of Lamu as keepers of the Swahili verse tradition" (Jahadhmy 1975, 28).

Prosodic developments in the Swahili verse tradition, however, were by no means limited to the *utenzi*. Indeed, by the turn of the nineteenth century, again under the impetus of the Afro-Arab contact, the entire Swahili poetic tradition had come under an elaborate prosodic system that governed the use of meter and rhyme. The golden period of Swahili literature, with poetry as its pivotal force, had been properly ushered in.

The nineteenth century, however, also saw the rise of a written poetic tradition that moved toward the secular. Everyday issues

of social and political importance were captured in verse and preserved for posterity in the Swahili-Arabic alphabet. The leading
spirit behind the popularization of this more secular poetic tradition was the inimitable Muyaka wa Mwinyi Haji (1776–1840), who
lived and composed in Mombasa on the coast of Kenya. Muyaka
marks the beginning of a gradual shift of the Swahili poetic genius from the northern coast of Kenya (Lamu and its archipelago)
to Mombasa, a shift precipitated in part by a conjuncture of new
historical and political circumstances in the region.

In the hands of Muyaka, the quatrain (or *shairi* in the Swahili
language) attained its rightful place as an important genre in the
Swahili poetic diction. The *shairi*, comprised of four-line verses, a
sixteen-syllable meter with a middle caesura, and a final rhyming
pattern, is often used for the more grave subject matter. Muyaka
produced *shairi* poems with an unmatched mastery on the topical
issues of his period. He wrote of love and infidelity, prosperity
and drought, the sexual exploits of key figures of his time, and
the calamities of the Mombasans. Above all, Muyaka became the
celebrated poet of the Mazrui reign of Mombasa in the first half
of the nineteenth century. And his war poetry, written during the
rivalry between Mombasa and other city-states, continues to ex-
cite the imagination of the Swahili to the present. In one of his
war-inspired poems, for example, he boasts:

> Ndimi taza nembetele, majini ndimi mbuaji
> Nishikapo nishikile, nyama ndimi mshikaji
> Ndipo nami wasinile, nimewashinda walaji
> Kiwiji samba wa maji, msonijua juani!

> Maji yakijaa tele, huandama maleleji
> Pepo za nyuma na mbele, nawinda wangu windaji
> Huzamia maji male, male yasofika mbiji
> Kiwiji simba wa maji, msonijua juani!

> I roam the seas, a hunter bold, in waters deep I slay!
> And in my fearsome grip I hold, relentlessly, my prey.

My foes would rend my flesh! Behold! 'Tis them I hold at
  bay!
For I am fierce and valiant, aye! The lion of the seas.

When high the surging rollers leap and squall, toss white
  the spray,
When back and forth the wild winds sweep, I hunt my
  hunter's way!
I sink in the depths of the water's deep, whose surge no
  ship may stay!
For I am fierce and valiant, aye! The lion of the seas.

(Translated in Gerard 1981, 103)

So central was Muyaka's poetry in the power struggles between
Swahili city-states during his time that scholars of his works liken
him to the court poets of Europe.

Muyaka's genius lay partly in his linking of the social relationship with the relationship of the ego. The poetry of the private
self is more limited in Afro-Islamic literature than it is in Afro-
European literature, but poets such as Muyaka helped build bridges
between individual privacy and public concern.

The secularization of Swahili written poetry within the traditional prosodic framework continued into the colonial period. In
the words of Gerard, "While Muslim subject-matter remained
paramount in Swahili literature, colonial enterprise fostered the
growth of a [new] trend . . . : the use of the epic forms for han-
dling secular topics and contemporary events" (Gerard 1981,
119). Of particular significance is poetry that sought to document
the colonial situation in what had become known as German East
Africa. Hemed Al-Buhry's *Utenzi wa Wadachi Kutamalaki Mrima*
(The Epic of German Rule of Mrima, 1955), Abdulkarim bin Jamaliddin's "Utenzi wa Vita vya Maji Maji" ("The Epic of the Maji
Maji War," 1957), and Mwengo Shomari's *Utenzi wa Mkwawa*
(The Epic of Mkwawa, which narrates the story of the Hehe chief
Mkwawa) are some prominent examples of this new poetic devel-
opment. Together, these three poems constitute an important

source of historical study and the sociocultural dynamics of this period of the history of Tanganyika.

The Swahili poetry of this period is at the center of an intellectual controversy that has been described in greater detail by Miehe, Bromber, Khamis, and Groberhode (2002, 87–89). The question has arisen as to whether the Swahili poets of this period reflected patriotic concerns against or in collaboration with the German colonial establishment. Arturo Jose Saavedra (forthcoming) suggests that in fact, terms such as *usaliti* (treachery) and *uzalendo* (patriotism) are a misnomer, given the historical context of the time. There was no notion of a nation as such rooted in any collective consciousness of the people, and different communities in the space that had come to be known as German East Africa responded and related to the Germans differently in accordance with their specific interests. Saavedra's study certainly takes this debate to new levels of intellectual challenge.

The classical Swahili tradition, however, continued to have an impact on the postcolonial period. The themes, style, and tone of Muyaka's poetry, in particular, have continued to influence modern poets such as Abdilatif Abdalla, Kaluta Amri Abedi, Zena Mahmud, Mwalimu Hassan Mbega, Khuleta Muhashamy, Ahmad Sheikh Nabhany, and Ahmad Nassir. Their poetry is replete with archaisms drawn from the work of poets who were contemporaries of Muyaka and earlier poets. One often needs a grounding in classical poetry to fully assimilate, appreciate, and evaluate their work. Swahili culture is so vital a component of their poetry that it is often difficult to dig into the nuances without some familiarity with the various registers of the Swahili language. Furthermore, the very fact that they have continued to compose on a variety of themes that are directly relevant to the realities of modern Africa has vindicated the assumption that modern themes and issues are capable of being versified within the traditional poetic diction. Their poetry is both classical and inventive without being stilted.

The public concerns of some of these poets are not only secular; they are also sometimes political. Abdilatif Abdalla is particularly renowned for his politically oriented poetry. Radical in his politics, he was imprisoned for supporting an opposition party in Kenya at a time when the political system was becoming increasingly autocratic. After a five-year term in jail on charges of sedition and libel, he compiled an anthology of prison poems that span his entire experience in Kenyan prisons. His poems are militant and unrepentant in tone. The sense of isolation and the effects of solitary confinement are vividly recaptured in the imagery he uses. The anthology is reminiscent of the poems of Muyaka that castigated the treasonable conduct of some of his compatriots. Equally striking is his nationalism. In one poem, which reflects on whether to embark on a self-imposed political exile by a finer flight of imagination, he puts himself in a position not unlike that of a crab: "Where else can a crab run save into its own shell?" (Abdalla 1973, 77).

In Tanzania, the tradition of composing poetry in conventional meter and rhyme received a particularly strong boost in recent times through the work of poets Kaluta Amri Abedi (d. 1964) and Saadan Kandoro (d. 2001). Both these figures were politicians of national repute, a background that enhanced their artistic clout and gave their poetry a nationalist orientation. Kaluta Amri Abedi is best known for his seminal prescriptive work *Sheriai za Kutunga Mashairi na Diwani ya Amri* (Rules of Poetic Composition and Amri's Anthology, 1954), which also carried a collection of his own poetry. Saadan Kandoro was an even more prolific poet and in 1969 was appointed the country's poet laureate by Tanzania's Academy of Letters. Like Abdilatif Abdalla's poetry, Kandoro's poetry has a strong magnetic resonance that captures hearts and minds. There is a sense in which Abedi's and Kandoro's advocacy of conventional meter and rhyme was part of their nationalist politics against foreign cultural incursions, a subject that will be discussed in greater detail in chapter 2.

Unlike many of the African poets writing in European languages, the poets writing in Swahili within the traditional prosodic framework are seldom groping for identity. There is a conspicuous absence of poems obsessed with cultural alienation or with cultural conflict with Europe or even poetry of the surrealist type. The only genre that comes closest to "alienation" is the so-called poetry of political combat. This includes poems that appear regularly in Swahili newspapers that are composed to condemn the evils of neocolonialism in its political sense and poems that recount the virtues of *ujamaa* in Tanzania. The poets themselves were trained in the classical Islamic education system and, in most cases, suffered only minimal cultural alienation. While the traditional Islamic system of education accommodated aspects of African traditional culture, the western system of education alienated and sometimes suppressed traditional value systems. The recipients of traditional Islamic education emerged equipped with both the Arabic alphabet and the roman alphabet and tended to use the two interchangeably. They became conscious of the existence of the legacy of Swahili literature before being initiated into the heritage of literature in European languages. They accepted the legacy of the *ulamaa*, the priestly poets of old, and at the same time searched for a new idiom commensurate with their time and place.

In their contributions to poetry columns in Swahili newspapers, these poets also seek to influence standards of language use in the society at large. The poets constitute an ipso facto Swahili academy, serving as the custodians of what they consider to be the very best of the Swahili linguistic tradition they seek to conserve and promote.

Closely related to the destiny of Swahili literature, however, is the development of the Swahili language itself. Even before the inception of European colonial rule, Swahili had managed to spread well beyond the frontiers of Swahili ethnicity and had acquired an important role as a medium of interethnic communication. But precisely because the language was still primarily circumscribed to trade functions, Swahili literature continued to be the exclusive preserve of people who were themselves ethnically Swahili. This status quo, however, was to be drastically transformed by the German invasion of Tanganyika in 1885 and the British colonization of Kenya, Uganda, and Zanzibar around 1895 as a new Swahili literature began to evolve from outside the traditional boundaries.

The earlier phase of this colonial linguistic history was virtually dominated by Christian missionaries who, inspired by their evangelical concerns, struggled to learn Swahili and in time rendered various sections of the Bible into the language using the Latin script. The missionaries were also initially responsible for exposing the West to Swahili literature by making its folktales available both in writing and in translation in European languages, and they introduced the West to Swahililand by having some English texts translated into Swahili. The Swahili versions of some of Charles Lamb's *Tales from Shakespeare*, Bunyan's *Pilgrim's Progress*, and *Aesop's Fables*, for example, were all produced during this early phase of the colonial dispensation (Rollins 1983, 113–14).

Later, the Germans broadened the use of Swahili and raised its status by making it the official language at the lower levels of their colonial administration. The British after them continued with this policy in Tanganyika and extended it, to a lesser extent, to parts of Kenya. But the British also went a step further by introducing the language into schools and encouraged its teaching as a subject in much of the Swahili-speaking area. They also promoted its use as a medium of instruction in lower elementary education throughout Tanganyika and Zanzibar—the two constituting what is today called Tanzania—and the native Swahili-speaking area of Kenya.

This new policy of Swahili as an academic language naturally placed the question of instructional materials for schools on the colonial educational agenda. An (East African) Inter-Territorial Language Committee was thus set up in 1930, partly to standardize the language and its new Latin-based orthography and partly to encourage local Africans to write creative works in the language. What came to be known as "Standard" Swahili was in the making based, supposedly, on the Zanzibar dialect of the language. Though initially opposed by the Swahili themselves, especially in Kenya, due to its seeming artificiality, the new imposed norm rapidly established roots in East Africa, especially among nonnative speakers. The orthographic Latinization of Swahili was also in full swing during this time and would gradually marginalize Swahili-Arabic writing altogether.

In their continued efforts to address the urgent need for classroom readers in Swahili, the British translated even more of their own literary classics into the language. From the late 1920s to the early 1940s, there was a proliferation of translated creative works that included Robert Louis Stevenson's *Treasure Island*, Rudyard Kipling's *Mowgli Stories*, Jonathan Swift's *Gulliver's Travels*, Rider Haggard's *Allan Quatermain* and *King Solomon's Mines*, and Lewis Carroll's *Alice in the Wonderland*.[2] By 1940, these British models in Swahili had sufficiently inspired the local population to stimulate new writing by East Africans themselves. These efforts were given further encouragement through the establishment of the East African Literature Bureau in 1948, which primarily focused on publishing Swahili-language texts.

European involvement in setting a new written norm for the Swahili language and its literature within the first half a century of colonial rule, therefore, was immense. According to Jack Rollins, "In terms of literary influence, one set of figures alone will explain more than several paragraphs. Between the years 1900–1950, there were approximately 359 works of prose published in Swahili; 346 of these were written by Europeans and published mainly in England and Germany. Many of these were translations: Swift, Bunyan, Moliere, Shakespeare, but none more pervasive, in more abundance, and having more effect than the Bible" (1985, 51). These biblical narratives in Swahili included not only the books of the Bible but also hymnbooks, catechisms, prayer books, and booklets on the lives of individual saints.

There were also Swahili newspapers of one type or another during the time of German rule in Tanganyika that sometimes carried short stories. *Msimulizi* (The Narrator) came into being in 1888 and *Habari za Mwezi* (Monthly News) in 1894. The two were soon followed by *Pwani na Bara* (The Coast and the Inland) and *Rafiki* (Friend) by the competing German Protestant Mission and German Catholic Mission, respectively. These experiments continued during the period of British colonial rule, initially under the impetus of British colonial administrators such as A. B. Hellier.

In his statistics, Rollins is unlikely to have included the works published by Muslim scholars such as Sheikh Al-Amin bin Ali Mazrui (1891–1947) and Sheikh Abdallah Saleh Farsy (1912–82). Nonetheless, the overwhelming proportion of the widely circulating materials produced by Euro-Christians, using what was conceived to be Standard Swahili, came to set the linguistic ideal by which East Africans, including the Swahili people themselves, were now expected to abide. The de-Islamization of Swahili, its ecumenicalization, was rapidly proceeding, a development that affected the destiny of Swahili literature in major ways in the decades to come.

But unlike the classical period of Swahili writing that emanated from the Kenya coast, the more modern phase of Swahili literature that was partly set in motion by the African-European encounter developed its strongest roots in Tanzania, where Standard Swahili was supposedly born. And while colonialism helped in consolidating the secular tradition in Swahili literature, it also impelled the emergence of new genres and subgenres, including prose fiction and written drama.

Prior to the colonial period, the only Swahili prose writing of significance was in the form of historical chronicles. The ones that were preserved include court chronicles such as *Tarekhe ya Pate* (The Pate Chronicle), which covers the years 1204 to 1885, and the *Khabari za Lamu* (The Lamu Chronicle), which covers the eighteenth and nineteenth centuries. There are also other chronicles that deal with the histories of Kilwa, Shungwaya, Mombasa, and other city-states. This genre continued to be encouraged by both the Germans and the British and set the background against which modern prose fiction emerged.

Following in the tradition of the chronicles was James Mbotela's *Uhuru wa Watumwa* (The Freeing of the Slaves, 1934) a semi-historical narrative that is widely regarded as the precursor of the Swahili novel. Though composed by an African, *Uhuru wa*

Watumwa is essentially colonial in its style, content, and ideology, to the extent that it exonerates the West in African enslavement.[3] But, as Albert Gerard notes, it is nonetheless important "for the history of Swahili literature because it exemplifies how a new trend was arising in modern-educated circles that were alien and even hostile to the predominantly Muslim and/or Arabic elements in traditional Swahili culture" (1981, 136).

The artist who is considered to have been most decisive in the development of modern Swahili writing, however, is Shaaban Robert from Tanga, Tanzania. Though a poet of note, his most important contribution to Swahili literature was in prose fiction, and his early writings are a clear demonstration of the multicultural heritage at work. His first novellas, *Kufikirika* (The Imaginable, 1967b, written in 1946 but published posthumously), *Kusadikika* (The Believable, 1951) and *Adili na Nduguze* (Adili and His Siblings, 1952) are all a fusion of a medium of composition of western influence and a stylistic tendency toward fantasy with a didactic orientation that expresses the legacies of both the African tradition and the *Alfu-lela-ulela* stories from the *The Thousand and One Nights*. In his later works, *Utubora Mkulima* (Utubora the Farmer, 1968a) and *Siku ya Watenzi Wote* (The Day of Reckoning, 1968b), however, Shaaban Robert moves closer to the novel in the western sense, making little appeal to the fantastic and having a multiplicity of plots and a large number of concrete characters clearly described in some depth and located more precisely in time and place.

Inspired by a strong sense of nationalism with a literary mission to raise the status of the Swahili language, Shaaban Robert is widely acclaimed for the colorful and rich quality of his language. And his renowned poem on Swahili continues to galvanize Tanzanians in their attempts to enrich the language in various ways. Robert urges his compatriots to cherish the language, for Swahili is to the Tanzanian what a mother's breast is to a child:

> Titi la mama litamu
> hata likawa la mbwa

Kiswahili naazimu
sifayo iliyofumbwa
Kwa wasiokufahamu
niimbe ilivyo kubwa
Toka kama mlizamu
funika palipozibwa
Titile mama litamu
jingine halishi hamu

Mother's breast is the sweetest
canine it may be,
And thou, Swahili, my mother-tongue
art still the dearest to me.
My song springs forth from a welling
heart, I offer this my plea,
That those who have not known thee
may join in homage to thee.
Mother's breast is the sweetest,
no other satisfies.

(Translated in Jahadhmy 1975, 3)

A Swahili of Yao origin (from Malawi), Shaaban Robert served
as a symbolic bridge between the Swahili and non-Swahili cultural universes at a time when Swahili literature was rapidly ceas-
ing to be an exclusively Swahili ethnic phenomenon. Its boundaries were expanding beyond the East African coast, beyond the
home of the Swahili where it was initially born. The trend toward
the de-ethnicization of Swahili literature in Tanzania was further
consolidated by the country's leftist move to *ujamaa*, a policy that
fostered the rise of Swahili as the national and official language of
the new East African state. But if the Swahili language and its literature had become de-ethnicized in a demographic sense, Tanzanian society itself was becoming increasingly Swahilized in a
cultural sense. The cultural label Swahili and the national label
Tanzanian were gradually becoming synonymous.

With his mastery of the language and his creative genius,
Shaaban Robert became a pioneer in the Swahilization of Tan-

zanian culture. His prose contributed to setting in motion a new trend in the Tanzanian imagination toward a transethnic Swahili literature. He clearly anticipated Tanzania's nationalist spirit, if not its revolutionary ideals. His was work that "expressed the views of a generation which saw the necessity for social changes but turned away from the road of violent revolutionary transformation" (Ohly 1985, 474).

But if Shaaban was the greatest inspirational figure in the emergence of Swahili prose fiction, it was his national compatriot Euphrase Kezilahabi who raised it to greater heights of artistic achievement. After the publication of his first novel, *Rosa Mistika* (1971), Kezilahabi quickly distinguished himself as a writer of extraordinary talent with the courage to test the boundaries of cultural censorship to address topical issues of social and political concern in Tanzania.[4] This trajectory is evident in his *Kichwamaji* (The Hydrocephalic, 1974a), *Dunia Uwanja wa Fujo* (The World Is a Stage of Confusion, 1975), *Gamba la Nyoka* (The Skin of a Snake, 1979) and *Nagona* (The Insight, 1987). More significant, it is Kezilahabi who placed the psychological novel firmly on the Swahili literary map, addressing, perhaps for the first time in Swahili prose writing, psychological themes such as alienation with vivid imagination. A product of university education both in Africa and the United States, Kezilahabi is described as "the greatest novelist of the Tanzanian mainland, who more than any other Swahili writer has been influenced by western literary trends" (Bertoncini 1989, 107). Some of his national compatriots have likened him to Thomas Mann and Albert Camus because of the existentialist orientation of some of his writings (Mlacha and Madmulla 1991, 31).

Representing almost the opposite trajectory is another equally accomplished writer of the modern period, Said Ahmed Mohamed of Zanzibar. University-educated in both Tanzania and Germany, Mohamed is a prose fiction writer, playwright, and poet, even though he is best known for his published novels—*Asali Chungu* (Bitter Honey, 1978), *Utengano* (Separation, 1980b), *Dunia Mti Mkavu* (The World Is a Dry Wood, 1980a), *Kiza Katika Nuru*

(Darkness in Light, 1988a), *Tata za Asumini* (Entangled Jas-
mine, 1990) and *Babu Alipofufuka* (When Grandfather Came Back
to Life, 2001). Like his celebrated compatriot Mohamed Suleiman
Mohamed—the author of *Kiu* (Thirst, 1972) and *Nyota ya Rehema*
(Rehema's Fortune, 1976), winner of the 1973 Kenyatta Prize
for Literature, and reputedly one of the most skilled Swahili
novelists of the twentieth century—Said Ahmed Mohamed has
demonstrated remarkable dexterity in language use and great in-
genuity in crafting the structures and plots of his stories. But
perhaps more than any other Swahili novelist, he was the writer
most strongly identified with socialist realism. His works have
a persistent focus on class exploitation and the class struggle.
As a result, he has sometimes been regarded as the Ngugi wa
Thiong'o of Swahili literature. In his latest novel, *Dunia Yao*
(Their World, 2006), however, he has decidedly shifted to the realm
of magical realism, which, in his opinion, provides him greater
imaginative and creative space (personal communication, March
30, 2003).

The works of Shaaban Robert, Euphrase Kezilahabi, and Said
Ahmed Mohamed fall under the larger taxonomic scheme discussed by Mlacha and Madumulla, who distinguish various types
of Swahili prose fiction: the psychological and the social, the historical and the political, the autobiographical and the ethnographic,
the utopian and the dystopian (Mlacha and Madumulla 1991,
29–43). There is also a rapid mushrooming of popular fiction, encouraged especially by the increase in the number of individually
and locally owned publishing houses. The earliest seminal figure
in this new Swahili fiction is the Zanzibar-born Mohamed Said
Abdalla, the writer of, among other novels, *Mzimu wa Watu wa
Kale* (The Ancestors' Graveyard, 1960), *Kisima cha Giningi* (The
Well of Giningi, 1968), *Duniani Kuna Watu* (The Earth Is Full of
Characters, 1973) and *Siri ya Sifuri* (The Secret of Zero, 1974).
This subgenre soon grew in leaps and bounds as Faraji Katalam-
bulla (1965, 1975, 1976) and others began to make their contri-
butions, with detective stories becoming particularly attractive.
And underlying all this growth and diversification of Swahili

prose fiction was an increasing tendency toward greater realism even as the oral heritage continued to exercise its influence, especially in matters of linguistic style.

A prose genre that has received far less attention than the novel has been the short story. East African Swahili newspapers such as *Mambo Leo* (Current Affairs), *Taifa Leo* (Daily Nation), *Baraza* (The Platform), and *Mzalendo* (The Patriot) seem to have served as the initial outlets for short-story compositions, going back to the early years of colonial rule. Later, beginning in the 1960s, *Kiswahili*, the official journal of the Institute of Swahili Research in Dar-es-Salaam, also began publishing Swahili short stories on an irregular basis. Anthologies of short stories, however, do not seem to have appeared until the early 1970s. An important stimulus in this direction were the Swahili short-story competitions that BBC Radio launched in 1967. Some of the submissions were later selected for publication under a series entitled *Hekaya za Kuburudisha* (Entertaining Tales), produced by Longman Kenya from 1970 to 1977.

A writer who has come to be recognized as one of the most gifted in this genre is the distinguished novelist from Zanzibar Mohamed Suleiman Mohamed. His stories invariably won the first prize in every BBC competition. With a general tone that swings between irony and humor, his stories are lyrical, full of suspense and surprise, and have characters that are rich and dynamic. Mohamed's creative genius in short-story writing was capped by his single-authored collection of six stories, *Kicheko cha Ushindi* (Laughter of Triumph, 1978).

Equally accomplished in this genre is another Zanzibar-born writer, Saad A. Yahya, best known for his collection *Pepeta* (Rice Flakes, 1973). Assuming the voice of a detached insider, Yahya explores with penetrating insight the various spaces in the complex lives of residents of Zanzibar (his original home) and Nairobi (his adopted home) in the postcolonial period. Weaving tragedy and irony, Yahya is an acute observer of the East African condition, and his collection is a demonstration not only of his creative genius but also his profound humanity.

At the heels of Mohamed and Yahya was their compatriot, the internationally acclaimed Said Ahmed Mohamed. Like Mohamed Suleiman Mohamed, Said Ahmed Mohamed made his initial appearance in the short-story scene through the BBC radio competitions. Winning several literary awards, his stories were among those that later appeared in the Longman series *Hekaya za Kuburudisha*. Said Ahmed Mohamed also took part in the short story competition organized by the Swahili service of Radio Deutsche Welle, coming at the very top in every instance. A selection of the latter stories eventually went into his anthology *Si Shetani si Wazimu* (It's Neither Spirit Nor Insanity, 1985). With his recent single-authored collections, *Sadiki Ukipenda na Hadithi Nyingine* (Believe It If You Wish and Other Stories, 2002a) and *Mfuko Mtupu na Hadithi Nyingine* (Empty Pocket and Other Stories, 2005a), he has arguably become the most prolific writer in this genre. More important, perhaps, his "Arusi ya Buldoza" ("Bulldozer's Wedding"), which appeared in his collection of short stories entitled *Arusi ya Buldoza na Hadithi Nyingine* (Bulldozer's Wedding and Other Stories, 2005b), places him in the rank of important pioneers of *uhalisiamazingaombwe*, the equivalent of magical realism in Swahili literature.

During this same period, Gabriel Ruhumbika produced his collection of four short stories, *Uwike Usiwike Kutakucha* (Crow or Not, Dawn Will Break, 1978). Varying widely in style from quasi-realistic to recrafted fables, Ruhumbika's stories are strongly didactic in their general orientation. But it is his compatriot, Alex Banzi, who seems to show even greater fidelity to didacticism and the traditional *ngano* (oral tale) in his choice of form, as demonstrated especially in his *Nipe Nikupe na Hadithi Nyingine* (Give Me and I Shall Give You and Other Stories, 1982).

Other distinguished writers of the short story include the poet Mugyabuso M. Mulokozi (who concentrates on political satire and quasi-revolutionary themes) and the outstanding and influential Swahili novelist Euphrase Kezilahabi (who emphasizes the existential). Their stories have appeared in several places, including newspapers, magazines, journals, and edited volumes, but neither of them has produced single-authored collections in this genre.

Kezilahabi's short story "Mayai Waziri wa Maradhi" ("Mayai, Minister of Diseases") constitutes the title of another collection of short stories by different authors that was edited by K. W. Wamitila (2004). Together, the eleven stories in this volume offer a critique of various dimensions of modern African society, from female candidacy in national elections to traditional healers and the AIDS pandemic, from the politics of food aid at times of drought to the excesses of Africa's leaders. Stylistically, as the editor himself suggests in the preface, the stories manifest features of the interface between orality and writing (2004, ii); they are essentially located at the hybrid space of Euro-African encounter.

A collection of short stories that is quite distinctive is *Mwandawazimu na Hadithi Nyingine* (The Insane and Other Stories, 2000), edited by Mwenda Mbatiah, who has risen to significant prominence as a Swahili creative writer. What distinguishes this text from most other collections is that the short stories have a unifying stylistic feature: they are all satirical in their depiction of the many social ills that afflict society, from corruption to child delinquency.

An important contributor to the development of the Swahili short story is Mbunda Msokile. Msokile too began by contributing his short stories to local newspapers. After experimenting with a couple of novelettes, he came to acquire special prominence as a short-story writer with the release of his anthology entitled *Nitakuja Kwa Siri* (I Will Come Secretly, 1981). But it is his extensive study of the short story, *Misingi ya Hadithi Fupi* (Foundations of the Short Story, 1992), that finally distinguished him as the most dedicated advocate of the genre. The first part of this lengthy text deals with theoretical and historical questions in the development of the Swahili short story. The second part is a vibrant collection of short stories by himself, Euphrase Kezilahabi, Mugyabuso Mulokozi, John Rutayisingwa, and Mohamed Suleiman Mohamed.

In spite of the many attributes that distinguish the stories of these various writers, however, most of them bear the unmistakable imprint of the *ngano*, demonstrating the affinity and synthesis between the "old" and the "new." In the majority of cases, it is impossible to tell where orality ends and the written begins in the continuing evolution of the modern Swahili short story.

The contribution of indigenous verbal arts to the development of Swahili literature is equally noticeable in written drama, even though the latter is more decidedly a product of the western educational system than prose writing.[5] Inspired by English dramatic works that were studied in schools during the colonial period, Swahili written plays first made their appearance in the late 1950s, beginning with *Mgeni Karibu* (Welcome Guest, 1957) by British expatriate teacher Graham Hyslop, and *Nakupenda Lakini . . .* (I Love You, But . . . , 1957), by Henry Kuria. Though this literary experimentation began in Kenya, it was in Tanzania that its greatest genius was to emerge, in the person of Ebrahim Hussein.

Hussein's career as a playwright covers virtually the entire spectrum of Swahili dramaturgical experience in the twentieth century. His first two plays, *Alikiona* (She Learned Her Lesson, 1970) and *Wakati Ukuta* (Time Is a Wall, 1971b), produced while he was still a student at the University of Dar es Salaam, were modeled on Aristotelian design. The frame of reference for these plays, as for many Swahili plays by other playwrights, is "a theatre that created and sustained Aristotelian illusion, that used a curtain or at least blackouts by electric light to mark or, more precisely, to conceal changes of scenes (scenery), and that, first of all, constructed a series of actions all leading to a single climax" (Fiebach 1997, 22).

This early postcolonial period was also one of growing cultural nationalism as African intellectuals sought to affirm an independent African aesthetic. In Tanzania this spirit of reculturation was further galvanized by the politics of *ujamaa*. And it is against the background of this political mood that Hussein produced his best-known drama, *Kinjeketile* (1969). Not only did the play center on a nationalist theme of historical importance, the

Maji Maji war against German colonial rule in Tanganyika, it also adopted Brechtian dramaturgy that was widely regarded as having a closer affinity with African performance arts than Aristotelian dramaturgy.

As an independent playwright, however, Hussein soon moved away from strict adherence to Aristotelian or Brechtian theatre. Instead, he tried to synthesize the legacy of the western theater and the tradition of indigenous arts. This is the dramaturgic trend that unfolds in his other plays, *Mashetani* (Devils, 1971a), *Arusi* (Wedding, 1980), and *Kwenye Ukingo wa Thim* (At the Edge of Thim, 1988). In particular, "Hussein discarded the illusionist components of received European artistic models" and in the process created a uniquely African drama out of Aristotelian foundations (Fiebach 1997, 28–29).

In the mid-1970s, Hussein also published two dramatic monologues, *Jogoo Kijijini* (Rooster in the Village, 1976) and *Ngao ya Jadi* (Shield of the Ancestors, 1976), which draw almost exclusively from the *ngano* and *kitendawili* (riddle) traditions of the Swahili. These and other works by Ebrahim Hussein are the focus of an excellent study by Alain Ricard (2000) that provides a complex analysis of the person and politics of this renowned African playwright.

However, it is Hussein's compatriot Penina Mlama (alias Penina Muhando)—the producer of *Hatia* (Guilt, 1972), *Pambo* (Decoration, 1975), *Nguzo Mama* (Mother Is a Pillar, 1982a) and *Lina Ubani* (It Has a Remedy, 1982b), among other plays—who has more consistently been associated with the African performance experience in her dramaturgy. Her plays have often been refreshingly sensitive to the different registers of the Swahili language and have quite successfully integrated song, dance, and ritual, adding to the Africanness of their theatrical form. Commenting on one of her productions, Micere Mugo has noted that Peninah "succeeds in this play, as few artists can, in engaging the emotions of the audience, so that they become completely and involuntarily absorbed in the fate of the characters. *Hatia* has an easy-flowing style, is arresting and commanding in effect, mainly because the playwright has such a tremendous capacity for creating suspense" (Mugo 1976, 139).

In the meantime, the appearance of Said Ahmed Mohamed's *Amezidi* (Gone Beyond the Limits, 1996), with its inclination toward an African theatre of the absurd, demonstrates the continuing potential of a multicultural synthesis in Swahili dramaturgy. Mohamed acknowledges the influence of Samuel Beckett's *Waiting for Godot* and Eugene Ionesco's *Rhinoceros*, *The Chairs*, and *The Lesson* on his composition of *Amezidi* (Njogu 1997a, iv). But there is little doubt, in the final analysis, that *Amezidi*, like Mohamed's earlier play entitled *Pungwa* (Exorcized, 1988b), is a hybrid of traditions that is peculiarly Swahili in literary experience.

In addition to prose writing and drama, East Africa's contact with the West also stimulated creative experimentation in written poetry as a new generation of poets sought to break away from the hitherto more strict confines of meter and rhyme. As discussed in greater detail in chapter 2, this development generated an intense and sometimes acrimonious debate among scholars of Swahili literature in East Africa.

Some of the practitioners of this emergent poetic genre, such as M. M. Mulokozi and K. K. Kahigi in *Malenga wa Bara* (Poets of the Uplands, 1976), Alamin Mazrui in *Chembe cha Moyo* (Arrow in My Heart, 1988) and Said Ahmed Mohamed in *'Sikate Tamaa* (Do Not Despair, 1980c), have sought to maintain a delicate balance between received prosody and free versification. The result has been the continued use of meter and rhyme but in a manner that is nontraditional and more flexible. Though still lacking in popular appeal, this new poetic style seems to have succeeded in establishing a certain degree of legitimacy within Swahili literature.

In all these developments within Swahili literature, women writers are grossly underrepresented. It is as if a de facto gender division has willed itself into the space of modern Swahili literature, with women as the main custodians of oral creativity and men as the main custodians of the written. Of course, this male dominance of written literature has not gone unchallenged. In drama, Penina Mlama continues to hold a place of great esteem.

In short-story writing, we are beginning to be exposed to new-comers such as Rayya Timamy and Rose Shake. And when it comes to the novelistic genre, N. Balisidya (*Shida*, Hardship, 1975), Angelina Chogo (*Wala Mbivu*, Eaters of Ripe Fruits, 1974; and *Kortini Mtu Huyu*, To Court, This Man, 1975), Zainab Mwanga (*Kiu ya Haki*, Thirst for Justice, 1983), and Amina Ng'ombo (*Heka Heka za Ulanguzi*, Activity of the Black Market, 1982) have made important contributions. But it is only Zainab W. Burhani, author of *Mwisho wa Koja* (The End of the Bouquet, 1997), *Mali ya Maskini* (The Poorman's/Poorwoman's Wealth, 2001), and *Kipimo cha Mizani* (The Weighing Scale, 2004), who has risen to become a writer of imaginative prose of regional repute. When all is said and done, however, it is still true that Swahili written literature betrays a disturbing gender gap.

Whatever the genre or the style, much of the modern literature—especially in prose and drama—tends to revolve around certain common themes of conflicting values. The most prominent of these is the conflict between tradition and modernity that, in most cases, is intertwined with the conflict between the rural and the urban. While some works idealize the traditional, others are critical of it or aspects of it, the difference sometimes being determined by the class background of the writer. Saad A. Yahya's short-story collection *Pepeta* (1973), Ebrahim Hussein's play *Wakati Ukuta* (Time Is a Wall, 1971b), Zainab Burhani's *Mwisho wa Koja*, and Mbunda Msolike's *Nitakuja Kwa Siri* (I Shall Come Secretly, 1981) all exemplify this thematic trajectory in Swahili literature. The theme of relations between men and women, especially in matters of love, sex, and marriage, has been especially productive as a topic for the exploration of conflicting values.

This same conflict, however, is sometimes presented in narrower terms as one between Africa and the West, between the indigenous and the foreign. This was particularly true of earlier writings that pitted Christianity against indigenous African religions, as in Samuel Sehoza's *Mwaka Katika Minyororo* (A Year in Chains, 1921). But other themes of conflict, like the indigenous versus western systems of education—for example, I. C. Mbenna's

Kuchagua (A Matter of Choice, 1972)—and indigenous versus western traditions of healing have been explored. In the realm of politics, examples of this thematic clash include Farouk Topan's *Aliyeonja Pepo* (The Taste of Paradise, 1973), J. R. Nguluma's *Chuki ya Kutawaliwa* (Hatred of the Colonized, 1980), O. B. N. Msewa's *Kifo cha Ugenini* (Death in a Foreign Land, 1977), and Mugyabuso Mulokozi's *Mukwawa wa Uhehe* (1979). And, in some rare cases, as in William B. Seme's *Njozi za Usiku* (Night Visions, 1973), the indigenous is presented nostalgically as a past that has been obliterated by western and modern encroachments.

The nationalist theme that seeks to recreate the anticolonial struggle that we find among Tanzanian writers (e.g., Hussein's *Kinjeketile* and Mulokozi's *Mukwawa wa Uhehe*) also has its corollary among Swahili writers of Kenyan origin, limited as the examples may be. Prominent among these are P. M. Kareithi's *Kaburi Bila Msalaba* (Grave without a Cross, 1969) and Peter Ngare's *Kikulacho ki Nguoni Mwako* (What Bites You Is in Your Clothes, 1975), which focus on the Mau Mau struggle against the British. Equally important, however, is the more recent novel by Mwenda Mbatiah, *Wimbo Mpya* (A New Song, 2004), which focuses on the postcolonial betrayal of the hopes and aspirations of the Mau Mau fighters for a new Kenya, one that is erected on the foundations of democracy, social justice, and the rule of law. In a sense, Mbatiah has begun to explore a theme in Swahili literature that has been at the core of Ngugi wa Thiong'o's creative work over the years.

The emergence of an educated class that has been influenced by the western liberal ethos and political ideologies has brought increased attention to the conflict between the individual and society in Swahili literature. Of particular concern is the location of the individual in modern African nation-states, where national unity is often promoted at the expense of subnational identities, or in more "traditional" societies that value collective welfare over individual rights and freedoms. The question of individualism features in many of Ebrahim Hussein's works, as Ricard (2000) amply demonstrates.[6] Euphrase Kezilahabi, on the other hand, has explored not only the problem of individual alienation (in his

Kichwamaji) but also the conflict between private property and the more socialist land tenure system wrought by *ujamaa*, as captured in his *Dunia Uwanja wa Fujo*.

The clash between individual rights and collective concerns brings us directly to the theme of conflict between socialism and capitalism. Unlike most of the other themes in Swahili literature that have been approached from a more "universalistic" angle, the concern with alternative politico-economic systems betrays greater regional variation. The socialist-oriented Swahili literature from Kenya, for example, is essentially a reaction to the country's more overt neocolonial reality. Said A. M. Khamis may be right that "most Swahili novels in Kenya written between the 70s and 90s follow a realist trend, but as a result of political inhibition and censorship, the majority of them are rendered apolitical, concentrating only on cultural and social issues" (2005, 94). But the few existing novels that draw from socialist inspiration tend to locate the possibility of radical change within the context of specific class tensions emanating from center-periphery relations tied to global capitalism. Mass class uprising (of the proletariat, the peasantry, or the petite bourgeoisie or some alliance[s] of these classes) is often depicted as the preferred strategy of revolutionary change. Katama Mkangi's satiric novels *Mafuta* (Grease, 1984) and *Walenisi* (The Damned, 1996), Rocha Chimerah's *Nyongo Mkalia Ini* (Pancreas, the Liver's Oppressor, 1995), and Alamin Mazrui's play *Kilio cha Haki* (Cry of Justice, 1981c) all fall within this domain of socialist literature to one degree or another. So does K. W. Wamitila's *Bina-Adamu* (Human Beings, 2002), which uses the village as a symbol of Africa to explore neoliberal relations of extreme exploitation between the West and Africa. The socialist trajectory in this literature is generally utopian in the loose sense of the word as an ideal to be aspired to, and the socialist system itself is not explicitly articulated.

The socialist-oriented literature of Tanzania is more rooted in experience. But we need to draw a distinction between the socialist literature of mainland Tanzania (or what was known as Tanganyika before its union with Zanzibar in 1964) and island

Tanzania (encompassing the islands of what was once the independent nation of Zanzibar). The socialist literature of mainland Tanzania is more explicitly inspired by the living experiences of members of *ujamaa* villages. Though some of these texts are critical of the excesses of their leaders or highlight practical problems in the process of formation and management of *ujamaa* villages, much of this literature seeks to demonstrate the socioeconomic and/or moral superiority of *ujamaa*.

Within this socialist tradition we have, for example, K. K. Kahigi and A. A. Ngerema's *Mwanzo wa Tufani* (The Beginning of a Storm, 1976), in which the domestic worker Kazimoto, who is exploited and abused by his employers, gains the sympathy and love of their daughter, Tereza; the two finally run away and find refuge and support in a socialist village. In John Ngomoi's *Ndoto ya Ndaria* (Ndaria's Dream, 1976), the leading character, Ndaria, is a rich farmer who uses every means at his disposal to prevent the introduction of *ujamaa* in his village of Ranzi. But once he noticed how flourishing a neighboring *ujamaa* village had become in a few years' time, he became guilt-ridden and subsequently did his utmost to turn Ranzi into an *ujamaa* village.

Along the same lines, in the socialist literature of mainland Tanzania, we find writings that support the ideals of *ujamaa* but are critical of the excesses of some of the leaders involved in the formation and management of the *ujamaa* villages. These excesses include administrative mismanagement, corruption, and forced villagization. Some of this literature also highlights more practical problems of socialism and the socialist construction of *ujamaa* villages without interrogating the validity of *ujamaa* ideals and claims. Examples of texts belonging to this category of critical *ujamaa* literature include *Kijiji Chetu* (Our Village, 1975) by Ngalimecha Nngahyoma, *Nyota ya Huzuni* (The Star of Grief, 1974) by George Liwenga, and *Dunia Uwanja wa Fujo* and *Gamba la Nyoka* by Euphrase Kezilahabi.

The socialist literature of island Tanzania, in contrast, derived its inspiration not from the lived experiences of *ujamaa* but from the bloody agonies of the Zanzibar Revolution of 1964. When *ujamaa* was promulgated as the politico-economic policy of the federated nation of Tanzania, Zanzibar was already on its revolutionary march toward socialism. As Kimani Njogu demonstrates, it is this revolution and its class background and precipitating conditions that have continued to inform the socialist-oriented literature of Zanzibar and Pemba writers such as Said Ahmed Mohamed and Shafi Adam Shafi (Njogu 1997b).

The important point to bear in mind here is that the road to *ujamaa* in mainland Tanzania, though it was pursued bureaucratically rather than democratically, was ultimately peaceful, enjoying much popular goodwill and meeting no militant opposition from antisocialist interest groups. The road to socialism in island Tanzania, on the other hand, was marked by a tremendous amount of violence. For historical reasons connected with "race" relations on the island and fears of attempts at counterrevolution, Zanzibar experienced an undue amount of bloodshed in its quest for a socialist order.

Against this backdrop, therefore, the socialist imagination in island Tanzania became virtually entrapped in a discourse of rationalization. Socialist-inspired writers of island Tanzania seemed to be under moral pressure to explain the basis and justification for the Zanzibar Revolution. They have sought to highlight the feudal-cum-capitalist relations of exploitation and the inhuman conditions of the life of the underprivileged classes in prerevolutionary Zanzibar. The impression is thus created that the magnitude of exploitation and oppression in prerevolutionary Zanzibar was bound to trigger a violent revolutionary upsurge with socialist aims. Mohamed S. Mohamed's *Nyota ya Rehema* (Rehema's Luck, 1976), Shafi Adam Shafi's *Kasri ya Mwinyi Fuad* (Lord Fuad's Palace, 1978), and Said Ahmed Mohamed's *Dunia Mti Mkavu* (The World Is a Dry Tree, 1980a) all betray this rationalizing tendency in Zanzibar's socialist-inspired literature.

In spite of its internal differences, however, much of the socialist literature of Tanzania has tended to omit references to neocolonial capitalism and dependency. This is a trajectory that clearly distinguishes it from the socialist-inspired literature of neighboring

Kenya. As indicated above, the socialist orientation of Kenyan writers such as the late Katama Mkangi, Rocha Chimerah, and Alamin Mazrui assumes the discourse of anticapitalist criticism of the neocolonial state. The focus on the homegrown system of *ujamaa* in mainland Tanzania and on the locally induced revolution at the dawn of independence in Zanzibar, in contrast, have relegated the problem of neocolonialism to the periphery of Tanzania's literary imagination in Swahili. But now that *ujamaa* has virtually been abandoned and the Zanzibar Revolution discredited, we can expect new trends in socialist-oriented writing in Tanzania. This possibility is clearly demonstrated by Said Ahmed Mohamed's play *Amezidi*, which explores, among other issues, the broader theme of Africa's dependence on the West.

Said Ahmed Mohamed is of the opinion that the Swahili novel has begun to show signs of radical transformation. The potential of this new trend is evident in Euphrase Kezilahabi's *Nagona* (The Insight, 1990a) and *Mzingile* (The Labyrinth, 1990b), Katama Mkangi's *Walenisi* (The Damned, 1995), Emmanuel Mbogo's *Vipuli vya Figo* (Kidney Trafficking, 1996), W. Mkufya's *Ziraili na Zirani* (Angel of Death and Zirani, 1999), and Said Ahmed Mohamed's *Babu Alipofufuka* (When Granddad Came Back to Life, 2001) and *Dunia Yao* (Their World, 2006). A hallmark of these novels, according to Khamis, is the attempt to dispense with the realist mode to one degree or another. In his words:

> With a realization that realism can never fully offer up the world in all its complexity and irreducible plenitude—especially in a new situation in which nothing is real as it used to be, some of the Swahili novelists embarked on a shift from a realist mode of writing with its illusory optimism and sometimes near linear chronological narrative order (though the two features are not inherently interconnected), to a mode of writing that warrants Barthes's designation of the "writerly" text that tends to be self-conscious, calling attention to itself as a work of art. (2005, 95)

Instead of the realism that has supposedly defined much of the novelistic writing in Swahili in recent years, we are now beginning to experience a new synthesis between the realistic and the bizarre (Khamis 2005, 102). As this transformation unfolds and as the people of the region become more aware of their common destiny under the politics of the neoliberal order, there may be a gradual convergence of thematic and stylistic concerns between Tanzania and Kenya.

In the meantime, the contrast between Kenya and Tanzania brings us to a fundamental anomaly of the East African aesthetic situation. It is Kenya, not Tanzania, that is the home of Swahili aesthetic genius at its richest. Most of the classical masterpieces of Swahili poetry came from the Kenya coast. The origins of Tanzania's contribution to Swahili literature are much more recent; they attained new heights of achievement only in the second half of the twentieth century. But the home of the older poetic traditions of the Swahili language and the source of most of the great epics was the Kenya coast. And yet in terms of general dissemination, Swahili culture is more widespread in Tanzania than in the Kenyan nation as a whole.

Among African countries, Tanzania has the fewest number of creative writers writing in English. The largest output in drama, prose, and poetry is in Swahili. The literature in general is a reflection of the nationalist character of Tanzanian society. Once the most radical nation in East Africa, it managed to decolonize the various aspects of life there, ranging from an emphasis on Kiswahili for legislative deliberations to the politicization of the so-called masses. Finding themselves in a radically tempestuous climate, poets and novelists also preoccupied themselves with the problem of "development." An entire state-sanctioned movement of *ngonjera* (dialogic and dramatic political poetry) has evolved to extol the virtues of Tanzanian nationhood and the pitfalls of too excessive a dependence on external cultural models. Day after day the predominant Swahili newspapers are inundated with poems that urge greater reliance on the land as the backbone of the Tanzanian economy and on the beauty of the Swahili language, customs, and political and literary culture.

Until recently, in contrast, the geographical area of concentrated Swahili aesthetic achievement in Kenya was more limited. Most of the country's noted writers came from the narrow coastal province. Outside this region, it is the Swahili language as a neutral medium of communication rather than Swahili culture as a rich vessel of heritage that had spread. It is now clear that this situation was only transient. As the language became more consolidated in the country, Kenya also began to realize the value of "nationalizing" the cumulative aesthetic accomplishments of the Kenya coast. In addition, the entire East African region continues to be in the throes of a cultural reappraisal that has received added impetus from the end of the Cold War, the entrenchment of global capitalism, the collapse of *ujamaa,* and the increasing pressure for pluralism. As these dynamics and counterdynamics continue to unfold, only the future can confirm their full implications on the destiny of Swahili literature and its multicultural heritage.

2

Aesthetics of Swahili Verse

Between the "Old" and the "New"

In June 1989, a Kenyan scholar of Swahili literature, commenting on my newly released collection of Swahili poems in free verse, declared that the kind of composition I had produced falls outside the realm of Swahili poetry and that it was at best a foreign poetry composed in the Swahili language (Ruo 1989, 21). Barely a week earlier, Mwenda Mbatiah had described the same collection as "a stylistic revolution," one that compared to the poetry of Christopher Okigbo, in which the "simplicity of form contrasts sharply with the complexity of themes" (Mbatiah 1989, 21). These two contrasting positions echo a debate between conservationism and liberalism in the Swahili verse tradition that goes back to the 1960s. I use the terms "conservationists" and "liberalists" to avoid the political connotations usually associated with the more commonly used terms "conservative" and "liberal." Conservationists are those who advocate the preservation of the poetic "status quo"—however we may understand that status quo—while liberalists tend to be advocates of experimentation with new poetic forms. The conservationist school is composed of people who range politically from radical to conservative. The liberalist school, whose exponents are mostly products of western-style schooling, includes within its ranks liberal-minded as well as left-oriented thinkers.

Needless to say, literary form and literary aesthetics may be deeply implicated in the question of identity. People tend to identify their literature not only in terms of its language and content but also in terms of the peculiarities of its form and style. As indicated in chapter 1, there is little evidence of the existence of the novel, the short story, the play, and free verse in their current manifestations in pre-twentieth-century Swahili literature. These genres and subgenres are more recent products of the encounter with European colonialism in the twentieth century. How did the Swahili respond to this infusion, much of it by colonial design, of new literary forms in their literature?

Interestingly enough, the Swahili never objected to the emergence of the novel, the short story, and the play in Swahili literature. These genres seem to have been regarded almost as organic extensions of the preexisting *ngano* and dramatic performances of *mashairi ya kujibizana* (dialogue poetry). But the introduction of free verse (and the less popular blank verse) quickly spurred the indignation of the Swahili intelligentsia. There are probably two underlying reasons for this response to the "new." First, between the *ngano* and the novel and short story and between dramatic poetry and the play there has been the difference in the very mode of presentation: oral versus written modes. It is an ironic fact of history that while the Arabic script was put to the service of poetic composition, it was not used in prose writing in the precolonial period. In a sense then, the novel, the short story, and the play came to assume a life of their own, separate from the normally unwritten *ngano* and dramatic poetry. But since there was already a long-established tradition of writing in Swahili poetry, the introduction of free verse in the written mode challenged the "stability" of the Swahili literary organism. As both operated within the written mode, free verse was seen to be in competition with the preexisting form of versification that combined meter and rhyme.

Second, writing tends to give its material a certain sense of immutability. People become much more passionately attached to the character of their written word because its seeming permanence enhances their sense of collective identity. When works of literature are written, maintained, and transmitted over several generations, the propensity for literary nationalism may deepen. As a result, a society may be less flexible about accommodating changes in its written literary tradition than it is about its oral literature. The Swahili have been less accommodating to changes in their written poetry than in their *ngano*, which have remained exclusively oral.

Against this backdrop, then, the strong reaction by sections of the Swahili people against free verse was to be expected. Theirs was an ethnonationalism of identitarian self-preservation. The terms within which this response was framed, however, produced a counterreaction that challenged the very genesis of Swahili "traditional" verse, leading to a debate that for a while polarized Swahili poetry into the individual components of its triple heritage: the indigenous tradition, the Arab influence, and the European impact. Two dimensions of this debate that came to assume prominence were the prosody and language of Swahili poetry. It is to a discussion of these aspects of the contestation that we shall now turn. The passions surrounding this conflict were sometimes so intense that they found intellectual release through poetic expression, making the medium of dialogue itself (verse) part of the message. Particularly instructive in this regard are a number of poems in Saadan Kandoro's collection (1978a).

There was a sense in which the introduction of free verse in Swahili poetry was projected as a liberating force from the "fetters" of rigid prosodic formalism. Breaking away from this Swahili poetic tradition was regarded as a bold and revolutionary pioneering act intended to liberate the full potential of the Swahili creative genius. It was probably a reaction to this contentious suggestion by the proponents of free verse that led Shihabuddin Chiraghdin to claim that the new mode of composition was prompted less by revolutionary zeal than by a sense of insecurity. The "new" poets had supposedly turned to a "foreign" creative style because they were not adequately skilled to compose in the traditional mode. According to Chiraghdin:[1]

Waliosema ati watu waliojaribu tungo za kigeni zisizo na funga-
mano lolote na arudhi ya Kiswahili ni mashujaa kwa kuwa ati
wameikata minyonyoro na kujitoa pingu za utungaji wa mashairi ya
Kiswahili, hawajasema lolote la maana, kwani mtu hutokaje katika
pingamizi za fani maalumu ikiwa kamwe fani yenyewe haimwelei?
. . . Hao wajigambao na hawana la kujigambia, wameambiwa tangu
kale:

Howe! Wapigaje howe, nyama usijamfuma?
Howe! Akali mwituni, na maguye mazima.
Howe! Nda mwenye kufuma, wewe una howe gani?

Those who claim that those who have experimented with foreign
modes of composition which have no relationship whatsoever with
Swahili prosodic rules are courageous because they have supposedly liberated themselves from the fetters of Swahili poetic composition have not said anything of substance, for how does one es-
cape the confines of a particular discipline when, in fact, (s)he has
no comprehension of that discipline? . . . Those who boast without having achieved anything to boast about have long been told:

Hooray! Why shout hooray when you haven't shot the prey?
Hooray! [When] it's still in the wild, with its legs intact.
Hooray! That's for the successful hunter; what is your cause
for celebration?

(1971, 13; my translation)

Chiraghdin thus likened the emerging free-verse poets to a hunter
who uses a blunt foreign weapon (English-style free verse) to hunt
a sophisticated and elusive prey (Swahili prosodic style), a hunter
who is boastful and jubilant without accomplishing his/her mission. To Chiraghdin, then, Swahili free verse was a nonstarter, a
foreign entity in the Swahili poetic organism that, though composed in Swahili, must be regarded as non-Swahili in literary
identity. Until recently, this was a sentiment that many Swahili
cultural nationalists shared.

Of course, Chiraghdin is wrong on virtually all counts. First, a
number of the proponents of free verse have demonstrated that

they can compose in the received prosodic style as easily as they can compose in free style; they have not proved inadequate in operating within the confines of meter and rhyme. In their compositions, some of them have even drawn from the same inspirational language and style of Muyaka as the conservationists have. Second, while the "new" poets may indeed find free verse liberating—a development that perhaps deserves a "hooray"—there is no evidence that they desire the demise of the received tradition of Swahili prosody.

Under these circumstances, Chiraghdin's statement must be read against the backdrop of new identitarian insecurities among the Swahili themselves. If there was anything in Swahili literary identity that had attained a cultural value of some permanence, it was the prosodic style of its poetry, the oldest artistic tradition that existed in written form. On the other hand, the proponents of free verse at that earlier phase seemed predominantly non-Swahili, and if they were Swahili, they were alienated products of western scholarship. What was essentially an experiment in Swahili free verse, then, was seen by Swahili ethnonationalists as yet another attempt to redefine the parameters of Swahili identity *from without.* The fear was that the parameters of Swahili identity were being set by "interest groups" other than the Swahili. It was an understandable, though by no means justifiable, reaction from a people who felt that their identity in the postcolony was under threat. It is this consideration perhaps that led Tigiti wa Sengo, in response to the claims of the liberalist school, to argue:

> Ushairi wa Kiswahili kama ulivyo ushairi wa Kingoni, wa Kinyamwezi, au wa Kimakonde ni urithi wa utamaduni wa watu wa jamii maalumu. Utaalamu wake utatokana na kukuzwa na utamaduni huo ama kwa kuukubali, kuuthamini na kujifunza kiasi cha kuwa na wewe watunga na kukubalika kuwa una kipawa cha utungaji.

> Swahili poetry, like Ngoni, Nyamwezi, or Makonde poetry, is the cultural heritage of a people of a specific society. Its mastery depends on either growing up in that culture or accepting it [for

what it is], valuing it and learning it to a point where one can compose and be accepted that (s)he has the gift of [poetic] composition. (1978, v; my translation)

According to Sengo, then, one becomes a Swahili poet after meeting the cultural and literary criteria developed over time within the Swahili community itself.

Saadan Kandoro goes even further in his objection to free verse. In spite of his own poetically articulated convictions that poetry "siyo vina na mizani" (is not rhyme and meter; 1978, 66), he relegates free verse to the realm of prose composition precisely because it does not obey the established conventions of meter and rhyme, concluding "Siyo insha mashairi, nakataa kataani" (Poetry is not prose, that I reject completely; 70). Kandoro thus not only dismisses the prosodic qualities of Swahili free verse but ignores the fact, which was especially well established in the *utenzi* tradition, of the linguistic symbiosis that obtains between verse and prose, between poeticity and narrativity.

In the same quotation above, Chiraghdin was also making the claim that Swahili free verse is foreign in origin, inspired perhaps by exposure to English poetry in the East African academy. The flip side of this claim is that preexisting Swahili prosodic verse is indigenous and, to some, specifically Bantu in its origin. In the introduction to his anthology of poetry by several poets, for example, Mayoka repudiates the free-verse anthologies of poets such as Kezilahabi, Kahigi, and Mulokozi in the following words:

> Katika kitabu hiki, tungo kama za Kezilahabi, Kahigi, Mulokozi na wengineo watungao tungo tutumbi zisizokuwa na sanaa yoyote nimezitupa pembeni. . . . Muundo wa mashairi yote yaliyomo kitabuni humu ni wa asili ya Kibantu.
>
> In this book, I have cast aside poems like those of Kezilahabi, Kahigi, Mulokozi, and others who produce many compositions devoid of any artistic merit. . . . The form of all the poems contained in this book is Bantu in origin. (1986, x; my translation)

This dual claim of Swahili ethnonationalists—that free verse is as foreign as "traditional" prosodic verse is African—naturally set off a reaction with a dual counterclaim. Pleading innocent to the charge of succumbing to the muse of English poetics, some advocates of free verse argued that on the contrary, it was Swahili's "traditional" verse that was inspired externally, in this case by an Arabic legacy. Those who championed the cause of prosodic poetry, therefore, were regarded as defenders, perhaps unconscious ones, of a poetics rooted in Arab cultural imperialism. As Mulokozi and Kahigi concluded:

> Kwa hivyo basi malenga wa Kiswahili wanaotetea vina na mizani hawatetei mambo ya msingi katika ushairi wa Kiswahili, bali wanatetea athari za Kiarabu, ijapokuwa kinafsi sio kusudi lao. Kwa kweli wengi wanaamini kuwa wanachokitetea ndio "uafrika."

> Therefore Swahili poets who advocate [the tradition of] rhyme and meter are not advocating anything foundational to Swahili poetry; rather they are advocating [the maintenance of] Arabic influence even though this is not their aim. In reality, many believe that what they are advocating is, in fact, the African tradition. (1979, 10; my translation)

Proponents of free verse further argued that Swahili free verse drew its inspiration not from English poetry but from African and specifically Bantu roots.

> Sasa je, ushairi wa mtiririko una asili ya Kizungu? Kwa hakika, dai hili la wanajadi lingekuwa sahihi iwapo mtindo wa aina hii usingekuwapo katika fasihi simulizi ya kibantu, ambayo ni pamoja na ile ya Kiswahili. . . . Mtindo usiofuata vina na urari wa mizani ni wa kijadi katika fasihi ya Kiswahili na kibantu.

> Now then, does free verse [in Swahili] have European origins? This claim of the traditionalists would have been accurate if this style [of composition] did not exist in Bantu oral literature, which

includes that of Swahili. . . . [But] the form that observes neither
rhyme nor meter is ancestral to Swahili and Bantu literature.
(Mulokozi and Kahigi 1979, 11; my translation)

To these scholars, then, the shift from the preexisting prosodic to
free verse in Swahili poetry was part of the struggle for cultural
decolonization, an exercise in the Bantu/African liberation of Swahili poetry from Arab domination.

Ibrahim Noor Shariff (1988), a staunch advocate of the conservationist school, responded from a very different perspective to the
claim of the *wana-mageuzi* (reformists or advocates of change, as
he calls them) that Swahili verse of indigenous (Bantu) origin did
not use meter and rhyme and that this prosodic practice in Swahili poetry today is a product of Arabic influence. Though Shariff
acknowledged and made no apologies for Arab and Arabic influences on the world of the Swahili, he insisted that there was less
than sufficient evidence to conclude that Swahili prosody is connected to Arabic poetic experiences. Even the earliest Swahili
poems on record, he claimed, were composed in meter and rhyme.
And to insist that the aesthetics of Swahili poetry could only
come from the Arabs is to deny the Swahili any independent
creative genius—even though, ironically, Shariff himself links
the more recent development of free verse to foreign (in this case
western) sources (201, 184).

Second, Shariff argued that Arab and Arabic influences on Swahili culture were part of a long and organic process, including intermarriage, that evolved over several centuries. It would be fu-
tile, argued Shariff, to attribute the quality of "foreignness" to the
unique synthesis that resulted from such a historical process.

Lakini [historia] ya Waingereza na Wajerumani ni kiyume na ya
waitwao Waarabu. Kwanza Wazungu hao wamekuja karibuni sana,
tena hawakuingiliana na watu kwa kuoana nao. Wamekuja kibeberu
na wameondoka bila ya kuwacha vizazi vyao. Na athari zao hasa
juu ya mambo yanayohusu lugha na fasihi na mengineyo ya mila
zao hayana mizizi katika mila za watu wa Afrika ya Mashariki ila
katika bongo za waliosomea shule za juu.

But the legacy of the British and the Germans is different from that of the so-called Arabs. First, the Europeans [in East Africa] are relatively recent arrivals and did not mix with the people by way of intermarriage. They came as imperialists and left without leaving behind their progeny. And their influence, especially on language and literature and other matters connected with their customs, has no roots in the customs of the people of East Africa except in the minds of those who received higher education. (1988, 195–96; my translation)

Thus, Shariff regarded the western heritage of Africa not only as less organic than the Arab-Islamic legacy but also as an expression of the mental alienation of Africans schooled in educational systems inherited from European colonizers.

When Shariff referred to Arabs as "so-called," he was leading to his third argument: the idea that at least some Arabs are African and that Arabic can be classified as an African language. He adduced both demographic and linguistic arguments to justify this conclusion.[2] In addition, he drew on the views of Bohannan that "geographically, the whole of the Arabian peninsula must be considered as unitary with the African continent" (1980, 42). If the demographic, linguistic, and geographic evidence suggests such an inseparable link between Arabness and Africanity, on what basis, asked Shariff, should we consider Arabic influences on Swahili as "foreign" to Africa? (Shariff 1988, 196–98). Even if one were to concede that Arab poetics influenced Swahili poetics, in other words (a position that Shariff did not accept), it must at best be seen as an intra-African phenomenon of cultural cross-breeding.

In the final analysis, the quasi-nationalist reaction and counter-reactions of both schools of thought led to a certain degree of purism, with each group claiming that its brand of poetry was more purely African than the other, more unadulterated by foreign influences than the other. The two views represented two sides of the same coin of nationalism that is blind to the historical forces that continually (re)shape human culture. It is difficult to say exactly when the meter and rhyme tradition began in

Swahili poetry, but there is no doubt that it was prompted, at least in part, by Swahili poets from the ranks of the Swahili literati, many of whom were deeply Arabized and influenced by Arab poetics. However, these influences stimulated the growth of Swahili poetry into a new synthesis that was still uniquely Swahili, and not into an imitation of Arabic poetry.

The same can be said about Swahili free verse. In spite of the claims of Mulokozi and Kahigi to the contrary, there is little doubt that English poetry in East Africa was the main source of its inspiration. Perhaps as a result of the debate between conservationists and liberalists, Swahili free-verse poets have also been under pressure to pay greater attention to the indigenous and oral poetic heritage of Bantu-speaking communities in East Africa. The resulting product has again been a poetic syncretism that is uniquely Swahili, a new fusion of the stylistics of orality and those of the written word.

In his contribution to this debate, Said Ahmed Mohamed had this rendering in free verse that appears in his anthology *Jicho la Ndani:*

> Kina, cha nini kina?
> Kina, sikitaki kina—iwapo chalazimishwa:
> > La kije kwa hiari
> > Tena kije vizuri
> > Kilingane na pumzi
> Zitazonifanya kuzamia kwenye vina na kuogelea.
>
> Rhyme, to what end rhyme?
> Rhyme, I have no need for rhyme—if it is imposed
> > Unless it comes spontaneously
> > And it comes naturally
> > In concordance with my verbal rhythms
> That will make me dive deep in rhymes and swim freely.
>
> (2002b, 78; my translation)

But poets of the conservationist school would argue that those who "force" meter and rhyme into their poetry do not deserve to be called poets at all. For in their view, the prosodics of meter and rhyme come quite naturally to genuine Swahili poets as a spontaneous verbal response to poetic inspiration. The problem, for them, is not with received patterns of meter and rhyme, it is with the popular misunderstanding that confuses poetry with nothing more than meter and rhyme.

Whatever the case, the status of Swahili poetry today, which is partly galvanized by the emergence of free verse, vindicates Farouk Topan, who in the early 1970s described the situation in the following terms:

> The choice of this form of composition, obviously influenced by modern English poetry, probably arises out of the desire of these young poets to react against the rigidity of the older but popular form. . . . It also reflects a sense of literary challenge on a fresh mode of composition. But that as it may, traditional scholars—staunch supporters of popular poetry—have already denounced this form as "non-Swahili." They fear that its acceptance as a bona fide form of Swahili poetry will not only dilute the composition of popular poetry but that it might even undermine it. . . . I find it difficult to accept [such] views; on the contrary, I believe that the acceptance of this modern form will enhance the status of Swahili poetry, enrich the genre, and widen the scope of its composition. (Topan 1974, 176)

It is interesting that Topan referred to the "traditional" mode of versification as "popular poetry"—suggesting, perhaps, not only that it was the more widely validated in the Swahili-speaking world but also that the new form was still the preserve of a new educational elite. But just as Arabic poetics once enriched Swahili poetry in new ways, the more recent western impact certainly enhanced the aesthetic value and the composition of Swahili poetry. In the process, it has now become quite common and even expected for anthologies of Swahili poetry to include rhymed, metered, and free verse. For example, K. W. Wamitila's edited volume *Tamthilia ya Maisha* (The Drama of Life, 2005), is a collection of poetry that includes compositions from as far back as the days of

Muyaka to the present and encompasses both poetry of the traditional type (Part I) and poems that dispense with traditional forms
of meter and rhyme (Part II).

In addition to the argument about local versus foreign sources
of Swahili poetry, there were also attempts to link the different
modes of versification with different modes of economic production. In particular, some liberalists portrayed meter and rhyme as
merely "decorative" devices of a dying feudal order that was inimi-
cal to the new forces of social and economic change that were taking place in the region. These liberalist scholars were clearly echo-
ing the Marxist proposition that culture (including aspects of art)
is a superstructure that is conditioned and shaped by the economic
base and economic relations of production. This view of meter and
rhyme in Swahili poetry was forcefully articulated by Mulokozi:

> Uozo na ubaradhuli wa maisha ya kumwinyi, hasa wakati mfumo
> huo unapoanza kutetereka kutokana na mabadiliko ya nguvu za
> jamii na uchumi, huwafanya mamwinyi, katika maisha yao ya
> kizembe na kifasiki, wapendelee sana mambo ya kuvutia macho
> na kuliwaza pua, kama vile mapambo ya aina aina, wanawake
> wazuri, nakshi na marembo ya rangi za kuvutia katika makazi na
> malazi yao . . . marashi na manukato, udi na ubani (na kadhalika).

The decadence and senselessness of feudalist lifestyle, especially
at a time when that order is beginning to crumble under the weight
of new social and economic forces, make the feudal aristocrats, in
their idle and immoral lifestyle, favor very much things attractive
to the eyes and soothing to the nose, like various kinds of decora-
tions, beautiful women, colorful adornments in their places of resi-
dence and rest . . . rosewater and perfumes, aromatic aloe wood
and frankincense (and so forth). (1975, 12; my translation)

And in complete agreement with Mulokozi, Senkoro wrote:

> Ni wazi kuwa baadhi ya washairi wetu wa Kiswahili wanaosisitiza
> mno kuhusu mapambo katika maana ya ushairi wanasisitiza tu
> mtazamo wa kimwinyi waliorithi vivi hivi tu bila kutambua asili
> yake.

It is clear [then] that some of the Swahili poets who insist on decorative devices [i.e., meter and rhyme] in the definition of poetry are simply advocating a feudalist perspective which they inherited and accepted blindly without being aware of its origin. (1988, 7; my translation)

Mulokozi and Senkoro's statements take the Swahili people, in the narrow ethnic sense of the term, to be the primary antagonists of free verse. They have singled them out, therefore, for a cultural offensive coated in quasi-leftist acrimony. In East Africa, it is the Swahili ethnic society that is widely known for its women who seek to dress attractively, to use aromatic compounds on their bodies and dress, and so forth. The use of "decorative devices" (of meter and rhyme) in the Swahili poetic body is now seen to belong to the same cultural orientation as the beautification of the human body, and the female body is once again the site of contestation. And it is that orientation that is described as both feudalist and decadent. In essence, then, rather than acknowledge the organic artistic interplay between substance and form, Mulokozi and Senkoro privileged the former over the latter.

At the time they were writing, Tanzania's experiment with *ujamaa* was still capturing the imagination of both Mulokozi and Senkoro. And it is possible that they regarded the debate between liberalists and conservationists as a contestation between feudalist aesthetics and socialist aesthetics within the political space of Tanzania. By the turn of the twenty-first century, however, the *ujamaa* experiment had been abandoned. Tanzania had capitulated to International Monetary Fund and World Bank conditionalities and joined the rest of East Africa in the web of neoliberal market forces. The result is a deformed capitalism throughout the East African region that has precipitated its own cultural and social problems: the increasing marginalization of certain sections of society, the growing feminization of poverty, the deepening of consumerist culture, the commodification of beauty, increasing sexual exploitation, and so forth. What will be the likely effects of these developments, which are the result of post–Cold War globalization, on Swahili literature? The situation is still unfolding.

In addition to meter and rhyme, the debate has also been concerned with the question of the language of Swahili poetry. If Topan considered "traditional" poetry to be the more popular poetry from the prosodic point of view, it is free verse that has been described as potentially the more popular from a linguistic point of view. This linguistic dimension of the debate is reflected in the liberalist charge that the language of Swahili "traditional" verse had evolved into a mode of discourse that was alien to the linguistic universe of the "common man." Liberalists also suggested that prosodic poetry had become the exclusive reserve of a conservative few.

> Ushairi wa Kiswahili umekuwa kwa muda mrefu mazungumzo kati ya watu wachache wauelewao au kikundi kidogo. Ipo haja ya kutelemka chini kwa watu wa kawaida na kuufanya utapakae.

For a long time Swahili poetry has been a dialogue between a few people who understand it or [between members of] a small group. There is a need for it to come down to the level of the common people and get to it to spread. (Kezilahabi 1974, xiv; my translation)

However, Cory, a British resident in what was then Tanganyika, anticipated Kezilahabi by some fifteen years. Having taken a liking to the popular Swahili verse that was published regularly in local newspapers, he was nevertheless bothered by the fact that he could not understand much of it, despite the fact that he regarded his proficiency in Swahili as approximating that of a native speaker. He sought the assistance of educated Africans who, he felt, might be more competent in the Swahili language, but to his dismay, he discovered that they fared no better than he did in deconstructing the idiom of Swahili poetry. Alarmed by this state of affairs, he remarked:

> Basi nilikuwa na wasiwasi, maana mashairi hayapasi kabisa kutungwa kama kwamba mashairi ni maarifa ya kufahamiwa na watu wachache walioelimika sana, bali yapasa yafahamiwe na watu wote

wenye maarifa ya kusoma na kuandika, pia na wengine wasiokuwa nayo. Labda mimi sikufahamu kwa sababu sikuwa na maarifa ya kutosha, au labda wale niliowachagua kunisaidia hawakufahamu vilevile. Lakini kwa vyovyote, nina hakika kuwa Mwafrika asiye na elimu nyingi ya Kiswahili haelewi wala kupendezwa na mashairi mengi ya Kiswahili yanayotungwa siku hizi.

So I became concerned, because poetry should not be composed as if it is specialized knowledge to be understood by an educated few; rather, it should be understood by all literate people as well as by those who are not literate. It is possible that I did not understand because my knowledge of Swahili was insufficient, or perhaps the people I chose to assist me also lacked the knowledge. But whatever the case, I am sure that an African who is not highly educated in the Swahili language cannot understand nor appreciate many Swahili poems composed nowadays. (1958, v; my translation)

For Cory, then, the problem was essentially a linguistic one that could be attributed to the impact of Arabic poetics on Swahili poetry. As a way of remedying the situation, he suggested that Swahili poetry needed to break from the Arab-Islamic tradition and allow itself to come under the influence of European literary forms (1958, vii). And as a step in that direction, he produced what may be regarded as the first anthology of free verse in Swahili.

According to the liberalists, then, the language of Swahili verse in the "traditional" prosodic style had become linguistically alienated from "the people" due to its semantic opacity, which created an impression that specialized knowledge and skill are necessary if one is expected to crack its linguistic shell in order to discover its semantic substance. If this was true, what specific linguistic features accounted for the semantic opacity that supposedly rendered it inaccessible to all but a select few? The proponents of poetic change and experimentation raised two objections to Swahili poetry of the classical pre-twentieth-century type. First, they regarded the frequency of linguistic Arabisms as evidence of a colonized mentality. Commenting on this tendency in pre-twentieth-century Swahili epic (*tenzi*) poems, Mulokozi writes: "This type of colonial mentality is, of course, reflected in the language. Some of the *tenzi* written at this time are so full of Arabic words and borrowings that it becomes impossible for one not conversant with Arabic to get their full meaning" (1975, 52). Ibrahim Noor Shariff responded to Mulokozi's argument by appealing to the notion of linguistic register. He observed that linguistic Arabisms are found primarily in poems with religious themes. Arabisms, according to Shariff, naturally have a special place in Swahili religious poetry because of the religious status of the Arabic language in Islam and in the community of Muslims (1988, 208–12). Shariff's argument, however, falls short of accounting for Arabisms in nonreligious poetry.

Second, liberalists objected to the use of "difficult words" in traditional prosodic verse. Fikeni Senkoro even suggested that this lexical aspect of the Swahili language of poetry derived from a "bourgeois" notion of the poet as prophet or some kind of human deity.

> Imani hii ambayo imeenea hasa katika nchi za kibepari ambako mwanasanaa ni mtu maalum asiye mmoja wa watu anaoandika juu yao, imepata nafasi kubwa sana katika kuipotosha nadharia ya Kiswahili. Kwa kufuatana na nadharia hii, baadhi ya washairi wa Kiswahili wameshikilia kutumia maneno magumu magumu.

This conviction that is most prevalent in capitalist countries where the artist is regarded as a special being and not from among the people about whom (s)he is writing has played a major role in distorting the entire perspective on Swahili poetry. In line with this perspective, some Swahili poets have insisted upon using difficult words. (1988, 6; my translation)

It is not quite clear what Senkoro means by "difficult words." The phrase apparently includes but is not restricted to linguistic Arabisms and seems to refer to "words" that are not within the "common linguistic knowledge" of the "average" Swahili speaker. The term would thus include words that are "jargonistic" or "archaic" and those that are confined to specific regional dialects.

Senkoro's claim that this linguistic trend in Swahili poetry emerged in response to the impact of a "bourgeois" notion of the artist is hardly justifiable in light of what we know about the more celebrated conservationist Swahili poets. Virtually all of them rose to prominence and some to elite status by the power of their own artistry and not by virtue of any influence of intellectual paradigms from the West. Unlike their liberalist counterparts, conservationist poets are akin to Gramsci's "organic intellectuals" in the sense that they emerged from the ranks of "the people" and not apart from them. As far as many members of the Swahili community are concerned, they and not the liberalists are the "people's poets," no matter how inaccessible their compositions might at times appear to be. They are genuine products of the Swahili intellectual environment and not offshoots of western cultural hegemony in East Africa.

The specific linguistic features under consideration are thus best seen not in terms of a western paradigm but historically in terms of the development of Swahili prosody in particular and the Swahili language in general. It is possible that at some point in its history Swahili verse was not bound by strict rules of meter and rhyme. At this time compositions were exclusively oral and performed in the "primary Swahili dialects" of respective composers (i.e., in those native dialects that existed prior to the recent spread of the language beyond its "original" coastal borders and certainly prior to the emergence of what has come to be known as Standard Swahili).

As the coastal people of Kenya continued to interact with Arab, Persian, and other African traders and settlers, Swahili language and its poetry evolved in a variety of ways. The more pronounced features of this evolution include the following:

1. Writing was adopted with a Swahili diagraph of Arabic (i.e., a modified version of Arabic orthography).[3] Writing opened the

way for experiments in poetic form—experiments that had not been possible in the oral mode.

2. Swahili writers became exposed to Arabic prosody. This external influence and the stimulus of writing complemented the internal dynamics of Swahili language and literature, leading to the emergence of a new Swahili prosody based on meter and rhyme. By the nineteenth century, a great classical tradition in meter and rhyme had become firmly established on the Swahili soil. This classical tradition so captured the imagination of the Swahili that it still exercises linguistic and formal influences on Swahili poets. Linguistic items and forms that were commonly used during the nineteenth century but are obsolete today continue to appear in the poetry of contemporary Swahili conservationist poets.

3. Islam expanded to a point where it became one of the defining characteristics of Swahili identity. This fact affected the linguistic destiny of Swahili poetry in two ways:

   a) The sacredness attributed to the Arabic language in Islam encouraged the use of unassimilated linguistic Arabisms first in the Swahili language and subsequently in Swahili poetry. In time, these Arabisms also came to be markers of upper-class status.

   b) With the spread of the religion came a new scholastic tradition, and the island of Lamu on the northern coast of Kenya established itself as the seat of Swahili-Islamic learning. For this reason, the Swahili dialect of Lamu gained prominence as the dialect of "high culture," as the de facto standard language of Swahili poetry, profoundly affecting Swahili religious and poetic discourse, especially in Kenya. This tendency was reinforced by the emergence of master poets from the ranks of the Lamu Muslim clergy, the *'ulamaa*. The use of linguistic Arabisms and Lamu dialect forms became most pronounced in religious poetry, but they also undoubtedly found their way into more secular Swahili poetry.

When the Germans and the British arrived in East Africa, they discovered a Swahili poetry that observed certain codes of rhyme and meter and was composed in the primary Swahili dialects of poets who occasionally made extensive use of unassimilated Arabisms, "archaisms" from the classical poetic tradition, and selected Lamu dialect items. These features had become an integral part of the wider aesthetic norm of Swahili poetry, a norm shared by the composers of poetry as well as the audiences that in most cases included the average, "common" Swahili people. This is the norm that many members of the Swahili community continue to associate with poetic diction to this day.

The Arab-Islamic impact spread the Swahili language beyond its original borders, but it generally played no more that an auxiliary function among the non-Swahili who acquired it as a consequence of trade activities in the region. Contact with Germanic-Christian civilization during the nineteenth century, however, prompted new dynamics in the development of Swahili language and literature:

1. Colonialism introduced new institutions and triggered a series of demographic shifts. In the process, schools, churches, and business and political activities became new venues for the acquisition of the language. If the Arab-Islamic impact initially contributed to the spread of Swahili in the marketplace, the Germanic-Christian influence helped diversify its functions among non-Swahili and introduced it into other spheres of social life. In the meantime, especially in Tanzania, "Swahili" became politicized into a national identity of the new nation-state. Furthermore, schools, churches, and the media exposed Swahili-speakers to a broader spectrum of Swahili literature.

2. A standard norm based on the Zanzibar dialect of Swahili was established. If the Lamu and, to a lesser extent, Mombasa dialects of Swahili had been developing spontaneously into standard norms due to religio-cultural reasons (which, of course, had politico-economic foundations), this process was

now subverted by the imposition of a standard form from above. The Swahili of schools, churches, and the media became variations of this standard norm, and much of the poetry of nonnative speakers of the language came to be composed in approximations of these historically more recent forms of Swahili.

3. The study of English literature in schools had the effect of exposing East Africans to a new kind of poetry; this experience later inspired experimentation with Swahili free verse and abstract metaphors.

The result of the above combination of forces was the expansion of the population from which Swahili poets could emerge and the generation of new aesthetic norms that were often in conflict with the more "traditional" Swahili aesthetic norm. The extreme positions in this conflict represented conservationism and liberalism. At one pole were poets who believed that they were composing for the narrow traditional "common" Swahili, who continued to be exposed to their respective primary dialects, Arabisms, archaisms, and "Lamuisms." At the other pole were poets who believed they were composing for the wider "common" non-Swahili, many of whom had not been exposed to these linguistic peculiarities of "traditional" Swahili poetry.

Social, political, and economic forces operating within the East African region now seem to have neutralized this polarity in favor of a new synthesis. For example, even among the most conservationist of Swahili poets, such as Ahmad Sheikh Nabhany and Ahmad Nassir, considerations of educational and market conditions have now influenced the linguistic dimension of their prosodic verse. The largest market for Swahili written verse in East Africa consists of students (in elementary and high schools) who are obliged to purchase books on government lists of required texts, and publishers are often willing to produce poetry that caters to this audience only. But precisely because schools favor Standard Swahili (or varieties that are close to it), all poets have been under increasing pressure to abide by the standard norm in order to have their poems published and adopted for use in schools.

In any case, the liberalists felt compelled to rebel against the conservationists' presumed linguistic position, for they were convinced that a major linguistic and prosodic revolution was required if Swahili poetry was to achieve its full potential for growth and development. Linguistically, this revolution was regarded as a break with the poetic diction of old and as an appeal for a more widespread use of the "common language of the people." As Kezilahabi declares in the introduction of his poetry anthology *Kichomi;*

> Jambo ninalotaka kuleta katika ushairi wa Kiswahili ni utumiaji wa lugha ya kawaida, lugha itumiwayo na watu katika mazungumzo yao ya kila siku. . . . Mapinduzi haya ya kutotumia vina na kutumia lugha ya kawaida ya watu yanatokea katika ushairi wa nchi mbalimbali. Nami nimefanya hivyo, siyo kuwaiga, lakini kwa kuwa naamini kwamba mapinduzi ya aina hii ni hatua moja kubwa mbele katika ushairi wa Kiswahili.

> What I would like to introduce into Swahili poetry is the use of ordinary language, the language used by people in their normal daily conversation. . . . This revolution of not using rhyme and using the ordinary language of the people has taken place in the poetry of many nations. And I have done so not to imitate them but because I believe that this kind of revolution is a major step forward in Swahili poetry. (1974b, xiii–xiv; my translation)

Kezilahabi's position constitutes a replaying of the Wordsworthian debate on African soil, a launching of Wordsworth's linguistic revolution in Swahiliphone Africa. This supposed linguistic revolution has meant a shift away from more localized dialects (such as Kiamu) to a dialect of wider communication (Standard Swahili in its many variations), a rejection of "archaisms" and unassimilated Arabisms, and a tendency to minimize the long-established poetic practice of lexical contraction (hitherto used mainly to fulfill metric requirements). As Kezilahabi saw it, this revolution would make Swahili verse less obscure and more semantically accessible, thus closer to "the people."

Of course, "linguistic proximity to the people" is a relative notion that depends on the poet's conception of "the people." Native speakers of Kimvita dialect (spoken in Mombasa) or Kiamu dialect (spoken in Lamu) grew up with the classical poetic tradition and were less likely to be alienated by the poetry of Nabhany, for example, than non-Swahili noncoastal Kenyans were. Part of the seeming linguistic problem, then, had to do with the kinds of audiences for which the two schools of poets were composing. But as the conservationists' own conception of their potential audience expanded to include nonnative and other speakers of Swahili, their language too began to undergo a transformation to become more easily comprehensible at the level of diction.

At the initial phases, however, this proposed linguistic shift in Swahili poetry was viewed with a certain degree of hostility by members of the conservationist school. They were not reacting so much to the use of approximations of Standard Swahili and the adoption of more current patterns of usage (after all, such poetry had existed before the emergence of the liberalist school); the conservationists seemed convinced, rather, that the traditional poetic idiom was threatened with subversion and ought to be protected if Swahili poetry was not to become stale and stunted. Thus, Chiraghdin argued that the acceptance of the emergent poetic form would mean that "kanuni zote za ushairi wa Kiswahili zitakuwa pindu pindu, vina vitakuwa havijulikani mwanzo havijulikani mwisho, na lugha yenyewe itakuwa chapwa au kuzidi. Na tungo hizo zikikubaliwa kuwa ni mashairi basi ushairi wa Kiswahili utakuwa umeanguka kitakotako" (all the fundamentals of Swahili poetry will be overturned, rhyme will be unrecognizable, and the language itself will be stale or even worse. And if these compositions are accepted as [Swahili] poems, then Swahili poetry will have fallen flat on its behind [my translation]; 1971, 14). Elsewhere Chiraghdin made an impassioned plea against confining Swahili poetry to a standard linguistic norm, which he feared would reduce its aesthetic efficacy (Chiraghdin, 1974, x–xii). To

the conservationists, the pan-dialectization of Swahili poetry and
the confinement of poetic diction to the popular could only dilute
the poetic power of the Swahili language. At that stage, the two
poles of the debate seemed irreconcilable.

The linguistic revolution advocated by the liberalists, however,
was by no means restricted to diction. It also encompassed the
level of metaphor, for some members of the liberalist school regarded "traditional" prosodic poetry as deficient in metaphoric
qualities. This alleged paucity of metaphor was in turn deemed
un-Bantu to the extent that "traditional" Bantu verse is rich in
metaphor. As Kezilahabi pointed out: "Mashairi ya wahenga wetu
yalikuwa yakiweka mkazo zaidi juu ya mafumbo kuliko vina na
mizani. Kwa hivyo uelewaji wa shairi ulikuwa uwezo wa kufum-
bua fumbo" (The poetry of our ancestors used to place greater
emphasis on metaphor than on rhyme and meter. Therefore, the
comprehension of a poem depended on the ability to deconstruct
the metaphor [my translation]; 1974b, xiv). Kezilahabi himself
supposedly sought guidance and inspiration from this Bantu
source for the metaphoric language he used in his collection of
Swahili poems, *Kichomi*. Even the title of Kezilahabi's collection
of poems has a metaphoric reading: *Kichomi* (literally "something that pricks/burns") suggests that Kezilahabi was conscious that his collection would provoke the indignation of the
conservationists.

In contrast, Topan discussed the special metaphoric quality of
Swahili free verse in terms of "symbolic imagery" whose aesthetic appeal lies in its potential to be interpreted in multiple
ways. For Topan, this attribute was more characteristic of the
new free-verse tradition than of the "traditional" prosodic verse.
In reality, however, it is not quite accurate to say that the pioneering efforts of free verse introduced metaphoric language and
symbolic imagery into Swahili poetry. What is true, perhaps, is
that metaphoric language in the emergent free verse tended more
toward the abstract and multiple ambiguity than the metaphoric
language in "traditional" prosodic verse. Thus, whereas liberalists found prosodic verse inaccessible in its diction and less

symbolic in its metaphor, conservationists regarded the language of the new free verse as wanting in expressive and poetic power.

When I taught university-level courses in Swahili literature in Kenya during the early 1980s, the students studied written poetry composed both in prosodic forms (in the classical tradition) and in free verse. Invariably they found the diction of the traditional verse less penetrable than that of free verse, and it is hardly surprising that many anthologies of metered-rhymed poetry contained glossaries to help readers understand unfamiliar terms and constructions. However, once the students had discovered the meanings of the lexical items in question, the poems became immediately accessible to them. In general, they experienced few problems in dealing with the types of metaphors used in "traditional" prosodic verse.

The situation was just the opposite with regard to free verse. Students tended to be more comfortable with its diction and rarely needed to consult glossaries or dictionaries to ascertain the literal meaning of words and phrases. Nevertheless, the new free verse was semantically less accessible to them at the level of metaphor. Although modernist aesthetics assumes that interpretation of metaphorical and figurative language is an integral part of literary appreciation, the experience with the first crop of Swahili free verse was often one in which literary appreciation was subordinated to the intellectual challenge of deconstructing its poetic metaphors.

The problem of semantic inaccessibility was already of great concern to readers of African verse in English, for which development Alain Ricard provides an interesting periodization—beginning with the pioneers of the 1950s, to early postcolonial poets like Christopher Okigbo (1932–67), through a new generation of the seventies like Oswald Mtshali (b. 1940), to the more recent poets of "new ethics" like Niyi Osundare (b. 1952) (2004, 145–53). Ali Mazrui (1967a); Chinweizu, Jemie, and Madubuike (1980); and Ayo Banjo (1983) all had occasion to discuss the "abstractness" of African verse in the English language and to point out the need to develop a poetic language that would make it more accessible to the "average" reader/listener. Mazrui later elaborated on his position when he was responding to some of his critics: "My objection to abstract verse was not that it did not allow for levels of meaning—but that the number of levels was infinite and undirected. The arbitrary sovereignty of the reader was given unlimited scope. There was no level at all at which the language of poetry and the language of prose converge to give plain intelligibility" (1975, 165). The shift recommended by these critics of abstract verse toward greater linguistic transparency was seen to reside within the literary space of African verse in indigenous African languages. According to some of these critics, "traditional African poetry speaks a public language" (Chinweizu, Jemie, and Madubuike 1980, 188), and modern African poetry in English was urged by them to seek inspiration in such indigenous models of versification.

But what was regarded as a contrast between African verse in English and African verse in indigenous languages also embraced the world of Swahili poetry. As indicated above, the debate about Swahili poetry was largely confined to diction, but in their quest for a new poetic order, liberalist poets composing in free verse replaced one kind of linguistic impenetrability (that of diction) with another kind (that of metaphor). They shifted from one level of semantic inaccessibility to another (perhaps more evasive) level. Ironically, what was intended to be "the ordinary language of the people" in Swahili free verse turned out to be as incomprehensible as the "specialized language" of classical Swahili poetry. If "traditional" Swahili poetry was accused of being a restricted dialogue within a small group of literary conservationists, free verse now assumed the character of a specialized discourse within a small circle of liberalist intellectuals.

Taken to its logical conclusion, the linguistic position of the liberalists was somewhat unrealistic. To expect the language of poetry to conform to "the language used by people in their normal daily conversation," as Kezilahabi suggested, was to expect language to contravene its very nature and betray its inherent dynamic variability. Language is a highly differentiated system, and poetry participates in the general sociolinguistic rules that apply to it. Unfortunately, liberalists confused the quest for linguistic accessibility in Swahili poetry with the attempt to make the language of poetry approximate that of the "common" person's everyday speech. In fact, in Swahili as in many other African cultures, poetic language was the ideal by which rhetorical speech in everyday communication was judged. As Ali Mazrui once pointed out:

> There is a school of thought in English poetry, represented by such people as Wordsworth and Coleridge, to the effect that poetry should approximate the ordinary language of conversation. But in Swahili culture there is a school of thought which would argue that ordinary conversation should try to approximate the elegant language of poetry. Those poems to the editor in Tanzanian newspapers, poems of dialogue, are part of this tradition. (1986, 244–45)

In other words, the earlier liberalist attempts to render Swahili poetry in the conversational register of the language would not only have been a negation of poetry itself but would also have constituted a reversal of Swahili linguistic values.

On the other hand, in a society where the poetic is often invoked in regular social interlocution, the boundaries between poetic language and conversational language are not always easy to define, and the two are in constant conversation with each other. Drawing on Bakhtin's notion of dialogism, for example, Kimani Njogu rightly points out in his contribution to this debate that

> the relationship between everyday speech and poeticity is one of mutual dependency and mutual reinforcement. It is a relationship informed by a simultaneity of presence and absence insofar as the poet approximates everyday speech and everyday speech approximates poetry with which it has come into contact. In their reciprocity, everyday speech and poetry influence each other both at the level of diction and subject matter. (2004, 76)

In any case, perhaps as a result of this debate—which was acrimonious at times—poets from both camps have increasingly moved toward both more penetrable diction and more penetrable metaphor as Swahili continues to impose its own course of development shaped by the mill of human experience.

In particular, Kimani Njogu identifies two dominant trends in the recent development of Swahili poetry. The first trend continues to exploit received conventions of meter and rhyme but in a manner that is more flexible, providing greater latitude for prosodic creativity. In reality, however, this trend can be described as new in the incidence of the practice rather than in stylistic orientation. In spite of the seeming rigidity of conventional Swahili poetry, it does in fact provide space for an unlimited range of prosodic combinations as long as the defining principle remains that of meter and rhyme.

The other trend Njogu discussed veers more decisively toward free verse but uses other verbal resources of poeticity. To exemplify this cautious tension "between metricity and nonmetricity, lineation and rhyme" in this category of poems, Njogu provides a deconstruction of Alamin Mazrui's poem "Muhibu wa Maisha" ("Eternal Love").[4] To appreciate Njogu's point, the poem and its English rendering by Njogu are reproduced below:

> Kwa nini . . . ewe nchi ulojipamba kwa weusi
>   ewe roho ya kizazi chetu
> tukutiliaye mboleya siku baada ya siku
> kwa kutaraji utatuzalia matunda ya umoja wetu
> Niambie . . .
>   Kwa nini ungali moyoni mwangu
>   Kwa nini ungali mpenzi wangu
>   katika saa hii ya huzuni?
>
>   Ni hii njaa na fisadi iliyotuzunguka
>   Au ni laana ya miungu iliyotufika?
>   Ni hasira ya nguvu nilovumbika
>   Au ni uchungu wa dhiki usiochinjika?

Nakuuliza kwa nini . . .
   Kwa nini ewe tamaa ya mtu mweusi
   ewe mashiko ya maisha yetu
   uloeneza mbegu za rangi yako duniani
   zikizaana katika uzao wa uhaini,
Nijibu . . .
   Kwa nini ungali ukinichoma moyoni
   kwa mahaba yaso kifani
   kwa nini ungali muhibu wangu
   katika saa hii ya huzuni?

Why is it . . . you, a land so well decorated by blackness
   You, the soul of our generation
We make you fertile day by day
hoping that some day you will reward us with the fruits of
      our unity
Tell me . . .
   Why are you still in my heart
   why are you still my beloved
   at this time of great sadness?

   Is it the hunger and corruption that surrounds us
   Or are we under a curse from the gods?
   Is it the anger of suppressed energies
   Or the bitterness of incessant agony?
I ask you why . . .
   Why is it, you loved one among the Black people
   You, who has spread out your seeds around the globe
   Multiplying under oppressive conditions
Answer me . . .
   Why do I still have sharp pangs in my heart
   for loving you so dearly
   why are you still my loved one
   at this time of great sadness?

                                        (Njogu 2004, 83–84)

In Njogu's opinion, this is an example of a poem that uses patterns in the form of repetition, pauses, and syntactic manipulation and its relation to lineation and perceived meter (which at times is standard) to reenact the disintegration and dissociation in the narrator's land. The metrical fragments and delicate rhythmic control contribute to our understanding of the total poem and the psychological state of the narrator (Njogu 2004, 83–85). And it is all part of the new experimentation toward a new synthesis in Swahili poetry, reflecting the hybridity emerging from the encounter between the East and the West in the crucible of African cultural production.

Elsewhere, Kimani Njogu offers his own interpretation of the underlying factor in the tension between the two schools of Swahili poetic thought, linking it to a wider debate between universalism and relativism. According to Njogu, the debate between the liberalists and conservationists "is allied to the apparent opposition between literary relativism and universalism. Whereas the 'conservationists' may be viewed as working towards a greater localization and cultural specificity of the confines of generic categories, the 'liberalists' may be perceived as lending towards universal points of reference" (2004, 76). Said Ahmed Mohamed essentially seems to agree with Njogu's interpretation when he suggests poetically:

'Lipopapasa walipo   wakaona metuwaa
Wakagundua vipapo   vina kwao vinang'aa
Wakang'ang'ania papo   pengine hapakufaa
          Hapo wakakoma
          Hapo wakasema
          Ushairi umekaa.

When they searched where   and felt comfortable
    they stood
And discovered them right there   rhymes shining bright
So there they held onto   Nowhere else was good
                                        enough

And there they stopped
There they then said
The poetic composition was complete.

(2002b, 72; my translation)

Advocates of traditional meter and rhyme, then, are depicted as parochial, stuck in their own cultural space and unwilling to explore the wider, universal horizons.

As Alidou and Mazrui (1999) have argued, the conflict between relativism and universalism in African literary discussions can be associated with the ideas of Benjamin Lee Whorf and Noam Chomsky, respectively. Whorf's views were influenced by those of his predecessor, Edward Sapir, and their contribution to linguistic relativism came to be popularly known as the Sapir-Whorf hypothesis. Sapir was not entirely consistent in his views about the relationship between language, culture, and cognition. In his earlier writings, he did not posit any particular correlation between linguistic form and cultural content. "When it comes to linguistic form," he declared, "Plato walks with the Macedonian swineherd, Confucius with the head-hunting savage of Assam" (1921, 134). Later, however, in his well-known article on the status of linguistics as a science, he took a deterministic turn, arguing that "human beings are very much at the mercy of the particular language which has become the medium of expression for their society. . . . The fact of the matter is that the 'real world' is to a large extent built up on the language habits of the group. No two languages are ever sufficiently similar to be considered as representing the same social reality" (1929, 209).

Whorf was an even more enthusiastic proponent of linguistic relativism than Sapir, for he claimed that a person's basic ontology or worldview is structured or determined or organized by language. Specifically, he argues that grammar embodies the nascent form of a cultural metaphysics. According to him, each language is encoded with a particular mode of thought, a metaphysics that affects the speaker's experience at the level of perception. For this reason he concludes that speakers of different languages will map the world in different ways; the linguist's task is to work out the fragments of a notional grammar (for example, categories of time, space, and gender) and determine the semantic associations by means of which it is translated into a cultural worldview.

Like Sapir, Whorf later modified his views and acknowledged that "the importance of language cannot . . . be taken to mean necessarily that nothing is back of it of the nature of what has traditionally been called 'mind.' My own studies suggest to me that language, for all its kingly role, is in some sense a superficial embroidery upon deeper processes of consciousness which are necessary before any communication, signaling, or symbolism whatsoever can occur" (1949, 239). Relativism thus subsumes a broad spectrum of opinions that range from a strong deterministic claim that language actually controls thought in a culturally specific manner to a rather weak suggestion that there is a loose correlation between language and cultural metaphysics. In spite of Sapir and Whorf's vacillations and those of other relativists, however, their rejection of a hierarchical ordering of language and their insistence upon the equality of cultures remained constant.[5]

In contrast, Chomsky stressed the common human features of language and played down the "surface" features that characterize individual languages. He declares, "It is plausible to suppose that apart from pathology (potentially an important area of inquiry), such variation as there may be is marginal and can safely be ignored across a broad range of linguistic investigation" (1986a, 18). Superimposed on this human linguistic uniformity is the assumption that the language faculty itself is an innate human characteristic. Chomsky views it as a genetically predetermined organized property of the mind and not an acquisition that is obtained from outside the individual by means of socio-psychological or cultural conditioning: "Knowledge of language is normally attained through brief exposure, and the character of the acquired knowledge may be largely predetermined. One would expect that human language should directly reflect the characteristics of human intellectual capacities, that language should be a direct mirror of mind in ways in which other systems of knowledge and belief

cannot" (ix–x). Chomsky thus supports one of the Enlighten-
ment's most cherished ideals—universal human identity.

In time, this linguistically founded dichotomy between relativism and universalism was extended to other disciplines, including literature, gender studies, multicultural studies, and the field
of human rights. What is clear, however, is that the two are not
mutually exclusive. It is not unusual for one to be invoked in support of the other. Daniel Arap Moi, the second president of the
Republic of Kenya, repeatedly exploited the universalist message
of cultural rights to defend a particularistic political order, just as
apartheid South Africa invoked the message of "different but equal"
to establish the edifice of Bantu homelands and Bantu education.

Njogu's application of the relativist-universalist dichotomy to
the debate between conservationist and liberalist in Swahili poetry overlooks this intersectionality of the two phenomena at certain cultural locations. Indeed, if there is a universalistic orientation
at all in the thinking of advocates of free verse, it has an ambigu-
ous expression, for Mulokozi and Kezilahabi and others repeatedly invoke relativist arguments and categories (such as Swahiliness, Bantuness, Africanity) to lend legitimacy to their liberalist
position. They deny the fact of literary hybridity to affirm a new
literary nationalist purism. Furthermore, relativism and universalism in the Swahili poetic debate are but two sides of the same
contested coin of intellectual class hegemony within the East African space.

Of all literary genres, poetry is the one on which the Swahili
seemed to have placed special value. Among the many features
that were used to determine the quality of poetic composition, they
regarded meter and rhyme as indispensable. The emergence of
English-inspired free verse in Swahili literature, then, was seen
as an open aggression against the aesthetic standards the Swahili
people had hitherto held sacrosanct. More significant, perhaps,
the Swahili saw it as an attempt to deny them an important expression of their collective consciousness and identity. To some
extent, the attempt to treat the emergent Swahili free verse as a
"foreign" mode of composition was part of a wider struggle for

self-preservation in a politico-economic context in which the Swahili people were beginning to feel marginalized and that their identity was being questioned. This defensive/protective dimension of Swahili ethnonationalism is discussed in greater detail by Mazrui and Shariff (1994).

Particularly conspicuous in this debate on the prosodics and linguistics of Swahili poetry was the absence of women's voices, a factor that can probably be attributed to the gendered hierarchization of knowledge and skills. Within the Swahili-Islamic tradition, the dynamics of patriarchy determined that writing and classical diction would be primarily the preserve of men, while orality and "vernacular" diction would be the domain of women. This gendered division in language and literacy is by no means absolute; it is rather relative. And because the legacy of women's verse in Swahili was oral and rendered in vernacular, women did not see the emergence of a new verse tradition in writing and in a new linguistic standard as a development that supplanted already existing forms of versification. Even when many Swahili women found the new verse form an oddity of a kind, they were often willing to see it as a parallel rather than a conflicting paradigm. In terms of their own poetic practices, then, Swahili women had little cause to oppose this poetic evolution in the Swahili literary space.

The literary debate must also be seen as emblematic of deeper shifts in power and class positions in the postcolonial dispensation. Throughout the precolonial period, the opinion-shapers—who reflected the interests of the ruling classes—were the Arabized male intelligentsia. This elite section of the population continued to enjoy more or less the same status under colonial rule partly because the Swahili coast as a whole was linked to the Zanzibar sultanate. With independence, however, elite status within the new nation-states was increasingly linked to "westernization," and "Europeanized" African writers began to draw from the western literary paradigm within which they had been trained. This shift explains why the contestation over Swahili prosody was at its most intense at the earliest phase of postcolonial history when the new westernized elite was seeking to inscribe itself in the Swahili literary space as the older and more "traditional" male elite struggled to maintain its age-old status. By the 1990s, the Arabized Swahili male elite had virtually been neutralized, both by the weakening of its politico-economic standing within the nation and by the relentless march of the western legacy even within the Swahili community itself. The young generation of the Swahili is growing up less and less familiar with the classical language of Swahili poetry. As a result, even the audience of traditionalist poets is gradually shrinking. This weakening of the "traditional" elite eventually led to the gradual death of voices opposed to free verse, allowing the new poetic tradition to acquire its own legitimacy within Swahili literature, which is increasingly fusing with pre-existing literary traditions to continue evolving in its uniquely Swahili style.

On the other hand, one notices that there is a marked difference between the poetic sentiments of the Swahili literary elite (of both the liberalist and conservationist orientation) and the poetic sentiments of the *mwananchi* (the common/average citizen). As with the division by gender, there has been a class division of knowledge and literacy skills. The *mwananchi* is predominantly a product of "vernacular" oral culture. As a result, any verse, free or rhymed and metered, can be aesthetically appealing to the *mwananchi* as long as it addresses her/his struggles, sentiments, desires, and experiences in a language that is plain, neither unduly abstract nor archaic, and in a style that can be subjected to the dictates and power of song and performance.

Just as the old literary elite has either been neutralized or assimilated into a new Swahili poetic ethos, it is true that the "traditional" mode of Swahili versification is becoming nationalized beyond the boundaries of Swahili ethnicity. One of the factors behind this cultural transformation is the sheer force of growing human intercourse fostered by both local and global dynamics in the region's political economy. Another factor relates to education: More and more students from various ethnic groups have the opportunity to study Swahili poetry, old and new, in schools throughout the East African region. Public school performances of Swahili poetry throughout the country are almost invariably in the classical tradition of meter and rhyme.

Yet another facilitator in the nationalization of Swahili verse relates to broadcasting and the *taarabu* tradition (a popular musical genre of multicultural origin). The most common broadcasting problems in Africa arise from the presence of many languages in the same country. Yet as Mazrui and Mazrui have argued (1998, 118–19), the problem could sometimes be one of having one language but different subcultures. In the 1950s in Kenya there were indeed radio programs in the Swahili language, but hardly any programs catered to the Swahili culture of the coast. It is true that only a minority of Kenyans speak Swahili as a native language. Yet it was precisely this minority that was not catered to in the broadcasting policy for some time prior to Kenya's independence. It was perhaps taken for granted that because those coastal people spoke Swahili, the national programs that were aired from Nairobi would meet their needs. Yet these were a people with distinct Swahili musical forms of their own, distinct Swahili poetry, distinct religious interests. The government radio programs at that time, though many were produced in Swahili, were directed mainly at nonnative speakers of the language in the interior of the country. The language was the same, but the cultural universe was different. And so Kenyans of the coast often tuned in to the Voice of Zanzibar, whose programs were culturally more akin to the interests of Swahili Kenyans than the programs from Nairobi ever managed to be in those days.

Laura Fair demonstrates that by this time, *taarabu* had already made its critical contribution to the consolidation of Zanzibar identity (2001, 171–75), an identity whose constituent attributes were widely shared by other Swahili-speaking peoples of the East African coast. She traces the origins of *taarabu* from its monarchic beginnings in Zanzibar to its appropriation by an Afro-Arab elite as the genre moved into the public sphere. At this time, the audience was still largely limited to the economic elite class. It took the legendary Siti binti Saad to revolutionize *taarab* and popularize it as an expression of a wider Swahili sense of belonging. In Fair's words:

> Siti binti Saad incorporated elements of both African and Arab sensibility into her life. As an artist she also creatively refashioned a number of already existing cultural and musical practices into a form that made taarab attractive to a cross-section of island society. Through her incorporation of stylistic elements drawn from the musical and performance cultures of the islands' Arab, African and South Asian residents, Siti crafted a musical space that widened the boundaries of "belonging." (175)

And through this hybridity, the identitarian boundaries of this artistic form crossed the islands of Zanzibar into other Swahili-speaking constituencies in mainland Tanganyika and Kenya. And once the Voice of Zanzibar was established, the magical voice of Siti binti Saad traveled through the electronic waves to its Swahili listeners throughout East Africa. This was a cultural experience that the Swahili-speaking peoples of the coast of Kenya could not get from within their country.

In the context of this broadcasting anomaly, a number of Swahili Kenyans themselves took initiative in the early 1950s in founding the Sauti ya Mvita broadcasting program from Mombasa. The colonial authorities encouraged them in this venture by first making basic broadcasting equipment and cable and wireless coastal headquarters available and later with other kinds of help and facilities. But essentially, Sauti ya Mvita started as a volunteer project by coastal Kenyans who felt culturally starved by radio programming in spite of the fact that their own language was used on national radio programs. These people shared a language with fellow Kenyans without necessarily sharing a common culture.

At Kenya's independence, of course, this media division was eliminated and all Kenyans were once again exposed to more or less the same media content. The new broadcasting service, however, also proceeded to embrace the magical power of *taarabu* songs and music. In time, the aesthetic accomplishments of the coast became more systematically nationalized. If *taarabu* was once heard only over the radio waves of the coast-oriented Sauti ya Mvita, it now became part of the national heritage and was played frequently on the national radio stations of East Africa. As Geoffrey King'ei rightly points out, *taarabu* has been appropriated by many East Africans who are not Swahili ethnically (1992, 44). Ntarangwi makes similar observations with regard to the appropriation of *taarabu* in Kenya by communities beyond the Swahili (2003, 163). This growing popularity of *taarabu*, which is often composed in "traditional" prosodic style and made possible by modern electronic technology, has aided the popularization of a culture of meter and rhyme beyond the boundaries of the Swahili. And as the Swahili language itself became more established, even the coastal poetic classics of the eighteenth and nineteenth centuries were accorded national status.

By catering to a more transethnic audience, *taarabu* has metamorphosed into something new. In seeking to explain this development in *taarabu*, Paul Musau has attributed it to new effects of globalization. Under the impact of globalization, he argues,

> instead of having one fixed and stable identity which is a function of predefined social roles, an individual has multiple selves and identities. . . . Accordingly, a *taarab* singer, or by extension a Swahili person, could be said to have multiple identities. At one time he or she could have the identity of the "traditional Swahili area"; at another time that of belonging to a larger geopolitical entity (e.g. Kenya, Zanzibar, Tanzania), while on another occasion he or she could have yet other identities. (2004, 188)

But to attribute the multiplicity of Swahili identity to the more recent (post–Cold War?) face of globalization is to ignore the fact that this identity has always existed as multiple and dynamic. As Mazrui and Shariff indicate, the question "What is your *kabila?*" could appropriately evoke any of the following responses that reflect different levels of consciousness of Swahili being—"Shikeli" (a member of the Shikeli clan—an intra-Swahili genetic consciousness), "Muamu" (a native of Lamu—an intra-Swahili geographical consciousness), "Mswahili" (a pan-Swahili cultural consciousness), "Mwislamu" (a Muslim—an extra-Swahili religious conscious-ness), "Mkenya" (a Kenyan—an extra-Swahili national conscious-ness), "Mwafrika" (an African—an extra-Swahili "racial" con-sciousness), or, for some, "Mwarabu" (an Arab—an extra-Swahili genetic ancestry)—all depending on the context in which that question is posed (1994, 6). In general, however, it is in the nature of all human identities that they are multiple, and which identity is salient at any point in time depends very much on the context and the situation.

Within the world of Swahili poetry, however, that multiplicity has long been circumscribed within certain boundaries of meter and rhyme. The emergence and gradual consolidation of free verse essentially shattered these boundaries and reconstituted them along new lines. Naturally, this development in Swahili poetry had an impact on how the Swahili people related to it as an ex-pression of their own ethnic identity. Today it is perhaps still true that Swahili poetry as a mirror of Swahili ethnic identity would be seen in terms of received meter and rhyme. But, as indicated above, the dynamics of the postcolony in East Africa has also eventually led to a certain coexistence between the two forms of versification, as Kimani Njogu so ably demonstrates (2004, 83–88). In time, this coexistence will evolve into a multidimensional syn-thesis, perhaps posing new questions about the interplay between poetry and identity in the Swahili imagination.

3

Religion and the Boundaries
of Swahili Literature

Much of pre-twentieth-century written Swahili literature, especially in its poetic form, could be described as Islamic, not only because of the subjects it treated but also because of the influence of the wider Muslim culture on canons of composition in East Africa. What Thomas Hodgkin said of Ghana's Islamic literary tradition is also true of the earlier stages of much of classical Swahili literature: "It is a literature which can properly be called Islamic in the sense that its authors were Muslim, trained in the Islamic sciences, conscious of their relationship with the Islamic past, and regarding literature as a vehicle for the expression of Islamic values" (1966, 442). It was full of didactic religious poetry, rendered in an indigenized version of the Arabic script, that called upon members of the Swahili society to live within the framework of Islam. Many of the poems were couched in religious terms, often derived from a wider Islamic tradition.

Some of the verse forms that emerged during this period, in fact, have continued to be used to this day among ethnically Swahili poets for themes that are almost entirely religious. These have included the *wajiwaji* and the *ukawafi* (compositions of five-line and four-line stanzas, respectively, fifteen syllables to a line and caesuras between the sixth and seventh and again between the tenth and the eleventh syllables) and the *inkishafi* (four lines to a stanza, ten syllables to a line, with a caesura between the sixth and seventh syllables). These types continue to defy any separation between form and Islamic substance. While the *wajiwaji* and *inkishafi* may be used for the composition of any religious theme, the *ukawafi* "deals exclusively with stories about prophets" (Shariff 1991b, 50).

As indicated by Hodgkin above, the fact that much of the poetry was composed by the *'ulamaa*, scholars versed in Islamic theology and jurisprudence, is also significant. Some were descended from a line of scholars, all with a high sensitivity to a spiritual relationship with the world around them. Many of these "lived and worked on the northern coast of Kenya . . . writing religious and didactic verse in the Arabic script and using one of the northern dialects of Swahili" (Whiteley 1969, 18). It is reasonable to assume that this *ajami* tradition in Swahili literature may itself have arisen out of a need to reach the common Mswahili spiritually through the effective medium of poetry. In the course of Qur'anic instruction, many Swahili acquired the capacity to read in the Arabic alphabet without the capacity to understand the Arabic language. *Ajami* became the bridge between the legacy of a foreign medium and literacy in an indigenous language.

One of the most prominent of these *'ulamaa*-poets is Sayyid Abdalla bin Nasir (1720–1820). A descendant of a long line of Swahili scholars, he composed the epic *Al-Inkishafi* (Self-Reflection) around the beginning of the nineteenth century. In the poem, the poet draws inspiration from the historical ruins of the island state of Pate on the coast of present-day Kenya and draws the analogy of death from them. By reflecting on the once accomplished and splendid achievements of the Swahili people of Pate, the beautiful architectural relics, the hedonist rulers, the intellectual life of the time, the poet castigates his own heart and urges it to take its cue from the fallen ruins and ephemeral nature of life. After describing the depths beneath and beyond the grave with terrifying clarity reminiscent of Dante's *Divine Comedy*, he warns his heart against taking this life seriously:

Moyo wangu nini huitabiri!
　　Twambe u mwelevu wa kukhitari
Huyui dunia ina ghururi?
　　Ndia za tatasi huzandamaye?

Suu ulimwengu bahari tesi,
　　Una matumbawe na mangi masi.
Aurakibuo juwa ni mwasi
　　Kwa kula khasara ukhasiriye

Why, O my soul, heed'st not thy future fate!
　　Soothly, if thou wert wise, discriminate,
Would'st not perceive this world of vain frustrate?
　　Why to its turmoiled paths dost ever turn?

'Tis as a surging sea, this mortal vale,
　　of found'ring reef and shoal of ragged shell.
Who rides it, as a tyrant knows it well
　　That loseth all to loss man's hoped-for gain.

(Hichens 1972, 65–67)

By verbal dexterity and touching imagery of pythons in hellfire, solitude amid ruins, he almost begs his heart to repent of its past sins and pray for the eternal peace and happiness that can only be found in the life after death. The Christian missionary-scholar W. E. Taylor may have been the first person to translate *Al-Inkishafi* into English in the late nineteenth century, describing it as "a great if not the greatest religious classic of the race" (see Stigand 1915, xi).

For all the innovations that have taken place over the years, the Swahili classical tradition continues to exercise its hold on the literary imagination of more-contemporary ethnic Swahili poets. As suggested in chapter 2, their poetry is replete with archaisms drawn from the generation of poets who were contemporaries of Nasir and earlier poets. Fully assimilating, appreciating, and evaluating their poetry often requires a grounding in classical poetry. Swahili-Islamic culture is so vital a component of this poetry that it is difficult to dig into the nuances without some familiarity with the various registers of Swahili as an Afro-Islamic language. And even some with a more secular orientation have continued to compose verse that is essentially Islamic.

Abdillatif Abdalla (b. 1946) stands out as one of the most prominent of modern poets. Currently a lecturer of Swahili at the University of Leipzig, he is best known for his collection of prison poetry, *Sauti ya Dhiki* (Voice of Agony, 1973), composed while serving a five-year jail term on charges of sedition in his native Kenya. In spite of the secular and radical political thrust of much of his poetry, Abdillatif is also a poet of the religious imagination. His *Utenzi wa Maisha ya Adamu na Hawaa* (The Epic of the Life of Adam and Eve, 1971), a 637-stanza verse in the classical prosodic tradition, is a critical account of "the fall" as narrated in the Qur'an. Reminiscent of John Milton's *Paradise Lost*, Abdillatif virtually sides with Hawaa (Eve), who accepts her humanness and seeks to live it to the full. And far from being the victim of the wily machinations of his partner under the influence of Iblis (Satan), Adam emerges as a figure robbed of his humanity by his seeming self-righteousness. Through this poem, then, Abdillatif inaugurated a new genre of critical Islamic literature—a departure from the otherworldly outlook of many a classical verse from Nasir's generation but still within the conceptual world of Islam.

There has been some debate, of course, on just how Islamic the Swahili literature of the nineteenth century and earlier periods was. As demonstrated in the following two excerpts—and these are not atypical of the views that prevail in the general run of scholarship on Swahili literature—Jan Knappert (1979) is of the position that the literature is immersed in Islam in its entirety:

> Swahili literature is profoundly immersed in its [Islamic] spirit. The Koran, the legends of the Prophet Muhammad and other prophets and saints of Islam, points of doctrine and theology are referred to on every page of traditional Swahili literature.

> Swahili literature, both prose and poetry, is full of references to Islamic law, and of admonitions to the faithful to observe it in

every detail. A knowledge of Islamic law is essential for under-standing Swahili literature, especially with regard to marriage and family law. (xix, xvii)

Tolmacheva questions the historical usefulness of the *utenzi* tradition because of what she regards as the wholly religious character of this subgenre (1978, 232–33). The privileging of the Arab-Islamic factor that prevails in discussions of the Swahili people and their Swahili language, therefore, also found its way into the study of Swahili literature, especially Swahili poetry.

Others have tried to demonstrate that at no point in their history did the Swahili produce a greater proportion of religious verse than secular verse. These scholars contend, however, that what ended up being documented in writing was overwhelmingly Islamic in orientation. Shariff argues that this tendency partly due to the fact that

> until the more recent days of German and British colonization in East Africa . . . the most literate among the Swahili were them-selves students, former students, or Islamic scholars who acquired their writing craft from the religious institutions. Hence, most of the scribes attached greater importance to the preservation of homiletic verse than of secular poetry. (Shariff 1991b, 41–42)

Assibi Amidou (1990, 3–4) and several other scholars have ex-pressed views similar to those of Shariff.

The rise to prominence of a Muslim clergy, however, led to a systematic bias in the preservation of the Swahili literary heri-tage. Poems that were more "purely" Islamic now stood a much greater chance of being preserved for posterity than those that were deemed to be less so in orientation. In the words of Amidou, "while the poems of Liyongo are much older than the Swahili version of the *Hamziya* and were probably written down long be-fore the 17th century, only the Islamic ones such as the *Hamziya* were approved of and preserved while the secular poems of Fumo Liyongo and his contemporaries were either suppressed or allowed to perish" (Amidou 1990, 4).

The Islamicist approach toward Swahili literature is rooted in two biases: a modal bias and a racial bias. The modal bias concerns the value accorded the written word. The written is given prominence over the oral even if the latter is more central in a given culture. Before the Swahili people began producing collections of their poetry in the Latin script, much of the so-called traditional Swahili verse that was secular existed essentially in the oral mode. I realize that it is not easy in "traditional" Swahili poetry to be specific about what would constitute nonreligious literature. Verbal discourse among the Swahili is often so saturated with phrases such as *Mola akipenda* (if God wills) and *rehema ya Mngu* (God's mercy) that it becomes difficult to draw a sharp distinction between the sacred and the secular in verbal culture. What may be secular thematically may be religious in ideological orientation. However, the scholars who suggest that Swahili traditional poetry is religious usually mean it in the thematic sense and not merely in terms of the use of words and phrases of religious origin. Bearing this qualification in mind, it is religious verse (in the thematic sense) that tended to be recorded or composed in the written word using the Arabic script, thanks largely to the orientation of the social strata that were the most directly engaged in preparing and preserving written documents. This literature, therefore, came to define virtually the entire scope of Swahili literature that came to be framed in quasi-Cartesian terms ("I write, therefore I am"), and what is unwritten is presumed to be nonexistent. By casting the indigenous oral tradition as underneath or even outside the "mainstream" literary discourses of the Swahili, the colonial project dismissed what was in fact the main stream of the time, which centered on orality.

The racial bias, on the other hand, operates on a hierarchy of racial types: European > Oriental > African. If the "Oriental race" is somewhat superior to the African race, then what is Oriental naturally becomes more preeminent and, therefore, more deserving of intellectual focus than that which is African. Hence, the African in Swahili literature became submerged by the undue focus on its "orientality." The modal and religious biases are not unrelated. The British colonizers, for example, generally tended to regard societies with a written tradition more highly than societies with an oral tradition alone. Together, the modal and racial biases of much of western scholarship conspired against Swahili literature's secular verse in favor of its Islamic compositions that supposedly betray its Oriental connections.

Within colonial discourse, of course, hybridity was a "dirty" word that was often associated with negative connotations and stereotypes. The Swahili people and their culture endured their share of disparaging projections on account of their hybridity. For example, Captain Stigand believed the Swahili combined the worst elements of their presumed dual heritage of African and Arab (Stigand 1913). Swahili literature, however, tended to reject this state of hybridity—even in its negative articulations—in favor of its putative "Arabic connections."

Some scholars, of course, have acknowledged that at least in the last century before British colonialism, traditional Swahili literature was not entirely religious. Commenting on the poetry that appeared in the local press in Tanganyika, for example, Lyndon Harries wrote:

> This wider modern practice of Swahili versification has led to a departure from its earlier intention to express the spirit and practice of Islam. Today the mechanism is employed for more secular ends. Any news item may be the subject of a few verses, but this is the tradition established during the nineteenth century by writers like Muyaka bin Haji of Mombasa, who brought poetry out of the mosque and into the marketplace. (1962, 2)

In other words, Muyaka (ca. 1776–1856) is regarded as the historical turning point of Swahili poetry: Swahili secular verse is presumed to have emerged during the "Muyaka era."

While Harries recognizes the emergence of secular poetry in the precolonial period, he continues to betray a modal bias. It is not clear how he could have drawn the conclusion that Muyaka was the first poet to compose secular verse. This view was probably influenced by the production in the *written* word of Hichens's edited collection of Muyaka's poetry. It is probable that the appearance *in print* of Muyaka's verse led to a sudden awakening that Swahili does indeed have a verse tradition that is not religious. And because Muyaka's was the first printed Swahili poetic anthology in the roman script, the tendency has been to attribute the beginning of secular poetry to him. In short, the modal bias has influenced views not only about our understanding of the history of Swahili secular verse but also about the longevity of the entire verse tradition of the Swahili people.

The contestation over the longevity of Swahili poetry is demonstrated particularly well in relation to the saga of Fumo Liyongo, the Swahili historical legend whose songs have been collected and published by the Liyongo Working Group in Germany (2004). Apart from being the earliest known hero in Swahili folklore, Liyongo is also regarded by the Swahili people as the earliest Swahili poet of note whose works are believed to have survived to this day. Just as the person of Muyaka became central to the debate on the longevity of secular verse, Liyongo came to personify the debate about the longevity of Swahili poetry in general. To the Swahili people, of course, Liyongo has meant more than this. As Shariff once wrote, Liyongo became

> an almost iconic representation of the depth, the achievement and the ambience of the culture as a whole. That he lived a thousand years ago, more or less, has come to symbolize the longevity of the poetic tradition as well as the early achievement of excellence within this tradition. That Fumo Liyongo was at once a major poet and a "hero" in the social world makes him, for the collective imagination, the embodiment of that combination of the poetic utterance and social practice which epitomizes the Swahili ideal of a fully developed human potential. (Shariff 1991a, 153–54)

The figure of Fumo Liyongo, then, was deeply embedded in the literary and cultural imagination of the Swahili people, and dating Liyongo became intimately tied to the historical consciousness and identity of this group.

The modal bias in favor of the written, however, has questioned the depth of this historical tradition, restricting its tenure to a period for which documentary evidence is available. For example, Knappert states that "it is probably safe to establish the date of Liyingo's death as 1690 or earlier. How much earlier will always remain a reason for controversy. Professor Freeman-Grenville places Liyongo about 1580. James Kirkman, too, believes that he may have lived around AD 1600" (1979, 66). This contrasts sharply with the position of scholars who have relied more heavily on the oral tradition. These include Chiraghidin (1973, 1) and Harries (1962, 6), who dated Liyongo's existence sometime between the ninth and thirteenth centuries. In essence, then, the difference of opinion centers on whether Liyongo existed earlier (i.e., during the pre-Portuguese period) or later (i.e., during the Portuguese period) in East Africa.

The issue of Liyongo's period of existence has implications not only for the longevity of the Swahili literary tradition but also for the religious constitution of the Swahili people. The Swahili are predominantly Muslim, and in their oral accounts they have all along regarded Liyongo as sharing in their faith as well as in their art. Islam has been such a central accompanying feature of Swahili identity that to claim that Liyongo was not a Muslim is to border on the claim that he was not ethnically Swahili. Such a claim, in other words, would disturb both the Swahili understanding of their culture and the collective consciousness of their history. If Liyongo lived sometime between the ninth and thirteenth centuries and if by then Islam had already become a feature of Swahili identity (Horton 1978, 88), it is inconceivable in the minds of the Swahili that Fumo Liyongo, their poet-hero, confessed a faith other than Islam. By historically placing him in the era of the Portuguese, Knappert created room for speculating that Liyongo could have been a Christian (1979, 68, see also 92) and not, as previously believed, a Muslim.

Ibrahim Shariff (1991a) was able to demonstrate, however, that the Swahili oral account is supported by archeological evidence presented by Mark Horton (1987) that places Liyongo before the fourteenth century, long before the inception of Portuguese rule and the Christian faith in East Africa. Shariff further argued that while the attempted "Christianization" of Fumo Liyongo rested on a misreading of certain aspects of Swahili history and poetry, it has sometimes been based on deliberate distortions and manipulation of literary information.

If the emphasis on Islamic literature is exaggerated, it is partly due to an Orientalist bias toward the written as opposed to the oral word, a bias that may have led to a confusion not only about the beginnings of nonreligious verse in Swahili literary history but also about the religious affiliation of Fumo Liyongo, one of its earliest poets on record. Yet it is true that much of the pre-twentieth-century written verse, on which Knappert and many others have tended to focus, is indeed Islamic in the sense defined above. It is in the oral domain of Swahili literature that we find an abundance of secular verse.

By marginalizing the oral, the modal bias also resulted in the marginalization of women's voices. The Muslim clergy that came to dominate and influence Islamic poetry in its written form were almost entirely male. The religious training of women seldom went beyond the performance and observance of certain core Islamic rituals. And because writing in the Arabic script was predominantly a male vocation, women's verbal artistry existed mainly in the space of orality and its thematic scope, which included a wide range of secular concerns. Of course, women poets such as Zena Mahmud of Lamu, Khuleta Muhashamy of Mombasa, and Moza Ali of Zanzibar composed both secular and religious verse in writing. But until recently, the examples of these women belonged more to a minority tradition than to the norm. The modal bias in favor of the written also amounted to a gender bias, relegating women's verse, which is often secular in nature, to the periphery.

But the story of the ecumenicalization of Swahili literature is founded on the spread of the language beyond its native Muslim population. In time, Swahili became a medium of worship and theology for Christianity and indigenous African religions as well as for Islam. Today, Swahili is the language of a Christian hymn, an Islamic sermon, and funeral rites in African traditional religions. Swahili religious concepts that were originally intended only for Islamic discourse have now penetrated the vocabulary of the Bible and of African initiation rites.

But in what sense was Swahili an Afro-Islamic language in its origins? Languages do not spring from other languages alone; they often evolve out of whole cultures and civilizations. It is true that Swahili is partly a product of the interaction between Bantu languages in East Africa and Arabic. But the impact of Arabic on the development of Swahili is part of the wider impact of Islam. The Islamic origins of Swahili partly lie in its readiness to borrow concepts, words, and idioms from the Arabic language and from Islamic civilization and partly from the fact that the influence of Islam once informed all aspects of the Swahili civilization. It is by no means accidental, then, that classical Swahili poetry is both part of the heritage of Africa and part of the universal legacy of Islam.

As the language of the Qur'an, Arabic is very susceptible to Islamic imagery and connotation. This helped enrich Swahili, as did borrowings from Bantu (and non-Bantu) languages of Africa. The word for God in Swahili (*Mngu*) comes from Bantu, whereas the word for angels (*malaika*) comes from Arabic. The word for heavens (*mbingu*) is of Bantu origin, whereas the word for earth (*ardhi*), especially when used religiously, comes from Arabic. The word for prophet (*mtume*) is from Bantu, whereas the word for devil (*shetani*) comes from Arabic. A wider range of illustrations could be added to these, showing an important interplay of meaning and symbolism between the universes of religious experiences in the traditions of Bantu-speaking peoples and the legacy of Islam (Mazrui and Mazrui 1999, 33).

The original alphabet used in writing Swahili also added to its Islamic image. Swahili has been a written language for over 500 years. Until the twentieth century, the script was based entirely on the Arabic alphabet with such modifications as were necessitated by the more elaborate sound system of the cross-cultural language of East Africa. The classical poems of Swahili, steeped as they were in Islamic tradition and imagery, were all originally written in this revised Arabic alphabet and preserved for posterity through that medium.

The ecumenicalization of Swahili began with its entry into the mainstream of formal education in East Africa, which came with European colonization and the infiltration of African societies by Christian missionaries. The great debate then began about the medium of instruction for Africans—the comparative merits of Swahili as against what were called "vernacular languages" and the comparative merits of Swahili as against the English language. This debate, especially when it touched upon the fundamental issues of educational policy, quite often became an issue between church and state in a colonial situation. It is to the ramifications of this grand dialogue, which is half religious and half political, that we now turn.

A rather simplistic but nevertheless suggestive distinction must be made between training the mind of the colonized African and converting his/her soul. Colonial policymakers in the administrative field at their most enlightened viewed education as a medium for training the African mind, but Christian missionaries viewed education as a method of winning the African soul. In reality, there was a good deal of overlap between these two concepts, and, in practice they were rarely sharply differentiated. But it is still true that the missionaries in those early days were especially concerned about "spiritual transformation," the elimination of "heathen tendencies," and the spread of the gospel. Secular colonial policymakers, in contrast, were interested in producing indigenous humanpower and legitimizing colonial rule to the outside world by providing education as an instrument of "modernization" rather than as an aid for spiritualization (Mazrui and Mazrui 1999, 70–72).

There were, of course, differences between German and British views on the Islamicity of the Swahili language. Prior to the revolutionary eruption of Maji Maji war of resistance, an important section of the German colonial establishment regarded Swahili as a reservoir of an Islamic spirit and a potential agent of interethnic African unity against German rule. According to one colonial ideologue of the time, H. Hansen, Islam and Swahili constituted not only the mortal adversaries of Christianity "but also, in Africa, the unrepentant enemies of colonial politics" (quoted in Pike 1986, 231). The existence of *El-Najah,* a Swahili newspaper that used the Arabic script and openly agitated against German colonial rule, was seen by sections of the German colonial administration as a vindication of Hansen's position.

On the other hand, Carl Meinhof, a prominent German linguist of that time who saw the adoption of Swahili as a very practical aid to German administration in Tanganyika, suggested that Swahili could be de-Islamized. Toward that end, he proposed replacing the Arabic script (which had been used for centuries in writing Swahili) with the roman script and Arab-Islamic loan words with Germanic ones (Pike 1985, 224). This linguistic strategy, he argued, would purge Swahili of its Islamism to render it a more suitable instrument of colonial consolidation.

It was in this political climate that German Christian missions (both Protestant and Catholic) began producing Swahili newspapers with the explicit aim of promoting the cultural foundations of German colonialism. These Kiswahili journalistic ventures of the late 1800s included *Msimulizi, Habari za Mwezi, Pwani na Bara,* and *Rafiki* (Mazrui and Mazrui 1999, 58). To further the ends of colonialism, then, the German colonial establishment did not consider it imperative to impose its own language. Rather, it was able to appropriate Swahili and make it the language of its media propaganda. This and several other examples from the British colonial experience demonstrate that inasmuch as the Swahili language served as an instrument of liberation, it was also very much a part of the colonial project of control and domination.

In the earliest days of British colonization and evangelism, the Christian missionaries did not hold the association of Swahili with Islam against the language. On the contrary, quite a few felt that since both Islam and Christianity were monotheistic religions that were drawn from the same Middle Eastern ancestry and shared a considerable number of spiritual concepts and values, Swahili would serve well for the conversion of indigenous Africans to Christianity precisely because it could already cope with the conceptual universe of Islam.

As early as 1850, the Rev. Dr. Johann Ludwig Krapf of the Church Missionary Society was campaigning for Swahili as a language of evangelism. In the eyes of Rev. Krapf, Swahili's status as a lingua franca and its rich reservoir of religious concepts relevant to Christianity made it an ideal language for East African Christianity. The only aspect of the language that Krapf found objectionable was its use of the Arabic script, which, if left to continue, would leave a wide door open to "Mohammedan proselytism among the inland tribes which may hereafter be Christianized and civilized" (Krapf 1850, 170). It was partly due to this fear that Krapf initiated the use of the roman script in writing Swahili. Otherwise Krapf is among the missionaries who both championed the use of Swahili for the Christian gospel and made substantial contributions toward the systematic study of the language (Mazrui and Mazrui 1999, 74).

By contrast, "vernacular languages" were deemed to be too saturated with associations and connotations drawn from an indigenous religious experience that was much further removed from Christianity than Islam was. Using these languages for Christian proselytism supposedly carried a risk of conceptual distortion greater than that posed by Islam. Bishop Edward Steere, a missionary of the Universities Mission to Central Africa (UMCA), concluded: "Neither is there any way by which we can make ourselves so readily intelligible or by which the Gospel can be preached as soon or so well than by means of the language of Zanzibar" (1870, ii).

For a brief while, Christianity was identified partly with knowledge of Swahili and the ability to read in that language. But as this identification grew, a new swing of opinion emerged. Certainly in Uganda, a movement to replace Swahili altogether with the major local language, Luganda, became quite strong. The Swahiliphile views of some missionaries came under increasing challenge, and the old association of Swahili with Islam was regarded as dysfunctional to Christianity. As Bishop Alfred R. Tucker in Uganda once commented about Bishop Alexander Mackay:

> Mackay . . . was very desirous of hastening the time when one language should dominate Central Africa, and that language, he hoped and believed, would be Swahili. . . . That there should be one language for Central Africa is a consummation devoutly to be wished, but God forbid that it should be Swahili. English? Yes! But Swahili, never. The one means the Bible and Protestant Christianity and the other Mohammedanism . . . sensuality, moral and physical degradation and ruin. Swahili is too closely related to Mohammedanism to be welcome in any mission field in Central Africa. (Tucker 1911, 262)

Similar sentiments were expressed in neighboring Tanganyika, then under German occupation, where Swahili was declared by some German colonial authorities to be so "irredeemably mixed with Islam that every expedient ought to be employed to obstruct their joint penetration" (Wright 1971, 113).[1]

By this time, however, Swahili had begun to make sufficient inroads into and enjoy the support of a sufficiently large constituency within the Christian community to continue having an expanding role in East African Christianity, in spite of the new opposition to it. Because of the pioneering work of missionaries, the roman alphabet rapidly gained ascendance in written Swahili. Today very few people even among the Swahili or other East African Muslims use the Arabic alphabet for the Swahili language. And with the instrumentality of this new script, the promotion of Swahili literacy skills became virtually normalized in Bible classes, especially in Kenya and Tanzania.

Within a couple of decades, Swahili writing in the roman script had become so established and so much a part of the colonial school environment that it began to cause ripples within the ranks of East African Muslim scholars. In 1931, for example, Sheikh Al-Amin bin Ali Mazrui, the distinguished reformist Muslim scholar from Mombasa, Kenya, complained that the roman script was not only inadequate for representing Swahili sounds but, worse still, it distorted the Swahili sound system. He argued that the orthographic Latinization of Swahili negatively influenced Swahili speech in a manner that violated its norms of aesthetics and sophistication. It increasingly transformed the language, divorcing it more and more from the rest of society. He suspected that the entire colonial project was intended to "de-Arabize" and, perhaps, "de-Islamize" Swahili. He wrote, "It is indeed a great loss on our part to speak this Swahili which has been tampered with by Europeans. Swahili is the language of the coastal people, and it is not pure except by its mixture with Arabic" (*Al-Islah*, June 20, 1932). Linguistic purity is usually conceived in terms of filtering out what is linguistically "foreign." But here was Sheikh Al-Amin celebrating a concept of purity based precisely on hybridity, the mixture between the indigenous (Bantu) and the foreign (Arabic), reemphasizing once again the perceived centrality of Arabic and Islamic civilization in the construction of Swahili. His was an ethnonationalism of selective hybridity that positively admitted certain world influences (Arab/Islamic/eastern) into the Swahili organism but determined to keep out others (European/Christian/western). And using his reputedly fiery paper *Al-Islah*, he urged his community to boycott this "school Swahili" that came with colonialism and the Christian mission.

In the final analysis, however, neither Christian reservations about the Islamicity of Swahili nor Muslim fears about its seeming de-Arabization in the hands of Europeans were sufficient to arrest the spread of the language beyond its traditionally Muslim borders. As European missionaries promoted Christianity they also sought to constrain the spread of Islam. Yet, ironically, they often used the Afro-Islamic language of Swahili to spread the gospel of Jesus. Even when some Christian missionaries preferred ethnic-bound languages to Swahili,[2] as they did in Uganda, they still looked to Swahili for neo-Islamic loan words. Thus, Swahili continued to expand its ecumenical role either directly or indirectly throughout East Africa.

As indicated in chapter 1, by the beginning of the twentieth century an entire body of written literature of the secular kind had developed, bringing the legacy of orality to the pages of the printed word. Side by side with this secularization of Swahili written literature, however, was the development of the ecumenical tradition. A pioneering figure in this new trend was William Edward Taylor, a missionary who lived in Mombasa, Kenya, in the 1880s and 1890s. His greatest contribution was his rendering of portions of the psalms into a Swahili poetic form that to some extent conforms to the received prosodic framework, as in his Zaburi I (Psalm I) below:

Yuna heri aso njama	Blessed is the one without intrigue
akenenda na wabaya	who does not go with the wicked
kiumbe aso simama	the mortal who does not stand
kwa ndia ziso lekeya	on paths that are not right
za wadhambi si za wema	of sinners, not of the good,
wala hajajikaliya	nor take his/her seat
na wacheka mambo piya	with those who laugh about everything
kwa kikao cha wabishi	in the abode of the quarrel-makers.

(Knappert 1979, 236)

This composition seeks to approximate the quatrain once popularized by Muyaka, even though the result is a rather stilted product.

But Taylor also reputedly ventured into new prosodic forms and new styles to make his verse more accessible to African converts, most of whom were not products of the Swahili Islamic culture and had had little exposure to the Swahili classical tradition in poetry. He tried to avoid the archaisms and Arabisms that characterized the more cherished poems among sections of the Swahili (Knappert 1979, 233–37). In the final analysis, then, Taylor introduced a poetic style that was alien to the Swahili Islamic ear, a style that laid the foundation for a characteristically Christian Swahili versification.

Taylor's work in Swahili verse was partly inspired by his zeal to convert the Muslim Swahili to Christianity. As a result of his missionary objectives, the Swahili were quick to versify their own reactions. Sheikh Al-Amin bin Ali Mazrui attributed one quite popular poem to Sheikh Salim bin Khalid Timamy in his unpublished *ajami* manuscript "Arudhi ya Kiswahili" ("Swahili Prosody"):

Usijizuzue u mtu mzima
Tela zindukana tena ujue
Ushike ibada ya Mola Karima
Sizue Tela Sizue

Yuwatangatanga na vyuo kwapani
Atafuta mema naye hayaoni
Ibada ya Mola haiko sokoni
Sizue Tela sizue.

Don't fool yourself, the adult that you are
Come to your senses Taylor and understand
And practice what the generous Lord has ordained
Don't fabricate, Taylor, don't fabricate

He walks around, books under his arm
Looking to do good which he cannot find
The good practices ordained by God are not in the
marketplace
Don't fabricate, Taylor, don't fabricate.

(my translation)

Ann Biersteker extensively discusses this poem and other poems composed by the Swahili in response to Taylor's hymns. According to Biersteker,

> The answer poems themselves appear to have been, in Bakhtin's sense, "parodies" of missionary discourse. . . . The poems do not simply reverse the terms of the discourse, although they do call for Taylor's conversion [to Islam]. Rather, [to use Bakhtin's categories,] they "introduce the permanent corrective to laughter" and

"a critique of the one-sided seriousness of the lofty direct word."
They offer "the corrective of reality," a "corrective" that is "rich,"
"fundamental," contradictory and "heteroglot." (1996, 234–35)

It is an irony of history, as Biersteker points out, that it is these
responses to Taylor rather than Taylor's own Christian-inspired
Swahili compositions that have survived in the records of the
Church Missionary Society (1996, 221).

Inasmuch as the missionaries applied Swahili to Christian texts,
however, they sought to make new infiltrations within Islam, to
penetrate the world of Islamic sacred literature. Most significant
was Canon Godfrey Dale's translation of the Qur'an as sacred literature in 1923, the first complete Swahili rendering of the Muslim Holy Book ever. A Christian missionary of the Zanzibar-based
Universities Mission to Central Africa from 1889 to 1925, Dale
made a special attempt to study and penetrate the "mind of Islam."
And the primary objective of his Swahili translation of the Qur'an
was to provide Christian missionaries with a better understanding of East African Islam in order to combat it better.

As one would expect, Muslim reception of Dale's translation
was a hostile one: the initiative was seen as a conscious Christian
invasion of an Islamic space. The fears and suspicions were reinforced by the claim that the translation was replete with errors in
the transfer of meaning from Arabic to Swahili and by the fact
that the translation was not accompanied by the Arabic original.
The absence of the language of the Qur'an in the text rendered it
less than authentic in the eyes of East African Muslims.

Desiring to limit the presumed damage caused by Dale's translation, Muslims were inspired to produce their own Swahili translations of the entire Qur'an. Sheikh Al-Amin bin Ali Mazrui was
the first to initiate this project, but he did not live long enough to
produce a published translation himself. It remained to his disci-
ple, Sheikh Muhammad Kasim Mazrui (1912–82), to continue
with his mission. Once the chief *kadhi* of Kenya, Sheikh Muhammad wrote books on the lives of the first four caliphs of Islam,
among other publications. He also wrote the widely circulating

Utumwa Katika Uislamu na Dini Nyenginezo (Slavery in Islam and Other Religions, 1976), which sought to counter the common association of Islam with slavery that had become part of the Christian anti-Muslim discourse in both colonial and postcolonial East Africa. But his most influential work was his Islamic periodical *Sauti ya Haki* (Voice of Truth/Justice), which popularized a Swahili-Islamic idiom based on the Mombasa dialect of Swahili, Kimvita. Indeed, Sheikh Muhammad believed that due to its greater phonological proximity with Arabic (real or imagined), Kimvita (among Swahili dialects) was best suited for a Swahili Islamic discourse.[3]

In the late 1970s, Sheikh Muhammad published the first four *suras* of the Qur'an, again in the Mombasa dialect of Swahili, and he had completed two others when he passed away in 1982 before their publication. But the Ahmadiyya Muslim Mission, founded by the nineteenth-century Indian religious militant Mirza Ghulam Ahmad, managed to publish a full translation in 1953 with a prologue that condemns Dale's translation and clearly demonstrates how Dale's work may have spurred the Ahmadiyya initiative. Ironically, however, like the Dale translation, the Ahmadiyya translation was also met with great moral indignation. One of the students of Sheikh Al-Amin bin Ali Mazrui, the renowned Sheikh Abdallah Saleh Farsy, proceeded to write a lengthy polemic refutation of the Ahmadiyya translation (1954).

David Anthony III has indicated that another complete translation of the Qur'an appeared in the same year as the Ahmadiyya translation. This was the work of Shaykh Abdullah Hasan bin 'Amir ash-Shirazi, "who was considered the foremost Shafi'i scholar in Dar es Salaam when he completed his manuscript in 1953" (2002, 26). What is not clear is the extent to which Shaykh ash-Shirazi's translation was intended to be a response to Dale. There is also no record that this translation was ever published.

In 1969, Sheikh Abdallah Saleh Farsy, then the chief *kadhi* of Kenya, produced his own complete Swahili translation of the Qur'an, in which many of his commentaries were a condemnation not of the alleged distortions of Dale but of the claims of the

Ahmadiyya translation. This polemical focus was perhaps provoked further by Ahmadiyya attempts to defend its own translation in a pamphlet by Ahmadi Shaykh K. A. Abedi entitled *Uongofu wa Tafsiri ya Kurani Tukufu* (The Correctness of the Translation of the Holy Qur'an, 1967). Perhaps the most prolific writer of Swahili Islamic books, Sheikh Farsy had by this time relocated to Kenya after the 1964 revolution in his native Zanzibar where he had served as the *kadhi* for several years. By the time he died in 1982, Sheikh Abdallah Saleh Farsy had produced over thirty Islamic publications in Swahili, ranging from the biography of Iman Shafi'i to a publication about the Prophet Muhammad's regular diet, from writings about the main differences between the various schools of Islamic thought to the biographies of the wives of the Prophet.

Equally significant perhaps was that the three sheikhs— Sheikh Al-Amin bin Ali Mazrui, Sheikh Abdallah Saleh Farsy, and Sheikh Muhammad Kasim Mazrui—were also poets in their own right. Sheikh Al-Amin not only wrote on Swahili prosody but composed several unpublished poems. One that has survived in the memory of some women to this day is his "Banati Zetu Banati" ("Our Girls"), which urges parents to provide educational opportunities for girls because it is they who will constitute the backbone of society. Sheikh Muhammad Kasim was also an accomplished poet. His "Wasiya" ("Will"), composed in anticipation of his death, is a very moving expression of his last wish and his sense of inner peace as he moves on to his next destination. Furthermore, his periodical *Sauti ya Haki* was an exercise in verbal artistry, often invoking the imaginative with a satirical tone to give maximum effect to his message. The pages of the periodical, whose circulation extended to Tanzania and Uganda, also served as a poetic forum, carrying verses by such distinguished figures as Ahmad Sheikh Nabhany and Zena Mahmud. The January 1981 and May 1981 issues of the periodical, for example, serialize Zena Mahmud's 44-stanza poem "Nasaha" ("Advice"), a critical interrogation of what she sees as the gradual degeneration of her society's moral order.

Sheikh Abdallah Saleh Farsy often punctuated his religious sermons with poetic recitation. The four-page preface to his Swahili translation of the Qur'an opens with a poem, closes with a poem, and is interspersed with poetry in the body of the text. He also produced many poems for different occasions, some of which appear in his biography (Musa 1986).

In short, then, the religious contributions of these scholars often included a contribution to Swahili literature, following in the footsteps of *'ulamaa*-poets of old. These include, among several others, Sheikh Abdalla bin Ali bin Nasir (author of *Al-Inkishafi*) and Sheikh Hemed bin Abdalla bin Said al-Buhry (best known for *Utenzi wa Qiyama, Utenzi wa Abdirrahmani na Sifiyani, Utenzi wa Kutawafu kwa Nabii,* and *Utenzi wa Sayyidna Hussein bin Ali*). Together, the body of poetic productions by these scholars helped galvanize the Swahilization of Islam in East Africa.

There was probably a time when the *Hamziyya* (in its Swahili translation and Arabic original) was a widely used text in Swahili mosques to celebrate the life of the Prophet Muhammad. In time, the *Mawlid* of Sayyid Ja'far bin Hassan bin Abdulkarim (Barzanjy) gained greater popularity, but mainly in its Arabic original. In 1966, Sheikh Abdallah Saleh Farsy produced a Swahili translation of the narrative (Farsy 1966). Later, Sheikh Muhammad Kasim Mazrui versified Sheikh Abdallah's translation. This version has now become the main text of *maulidi* (Prophet Muhammad's birthday) celebrations of the association of women of the Islamic Center (Mombasa). And like all *maulidi* celebrations, the Islamic Center's annual event is interspersed with several Swahili *kasida* (religious songs) on the attributes of the Prophet Muhammad.

Even as Christian missionaries tried to invade the Islamic space, however, they continued to inscribe the Euro-Christian literary tradition on the shores of East Africa through Swahili translation of European classics, from Bunyan to the Bible. According to Rollins, translations of the Bible by Europeans constituted the largest portion of Swahili publication between 1900 and 1950. Rollins further adds:

The British and Foreign Bible Archives in London show that thousands of copies of either books from the Bible, or the entire Bible itself had been distributed in East Africa by the turn of the century. A common yearly run was between 5–10,000 copies. This is not to mention the many editions of individual hymn books, catechisms, prayer books, lives of saints and so on that also quickly found their way into Swahili by the beginning of the 20th century. (1985, 51)

This outpouring of Christian-inspired publications is a good measure of how rapidly Swahili language and literature were entering the ecumenical stage of their historical development.

It was not until the 1960s that East Africans, rather than Europeans, began to gain some prominence in compositions of Christian orientation. Pioneering among these was Mathias Mnyampala (1919–1969), a devout Roman Catholic of Tanzanian origin to whom Swahili was a second language. Unlike his European predecessors, who sought to Europeanize Swahili verse to accommodate their Euro-Christian tastes, Mnyampala composed in the classical tradition of the Muslim *'ulamaa*. His was a poetry that was still "Islamic" in form but Christian in content. As seen below, his *Utenzi wa Enjili Takatifu* (Epic of the Holy Gospel) followed the Islamic liturgical tradition of *tenzi*—four-line verses with eight syllables to a line and an aaab rhyming pattern.

Mungu unipe wajio	God, give me instruction
nitowe masimulio	that I may give my narration
nitimize kusudio	that I may accomplish my purpose
la Enjili kusifia	of praising the Gospel
Nasifia utukufu	I will appraise the honor
Mandiko matakatifu	of the Holy Scriptures
Mungu wetu kumsifu	(And) to praise our God
Mwana nae Roho pia.	the Son as well as the Holy Spirit.

(Knappert 1979, 276)

In spite of his allegiance to the local linguistic and literary traditions of Afro-Islam, however, Mnyampala is said to have been "closer to European or western thought since he had the outlook of a Christian" in many important ways (Knappert 1979, 272–73).

There have been several republications of Swahili collections of Christian hymns. Some of these bear the names but not the prosodics of conventional Swahili poetry. A hymn collection of the Tanganyika Mennonite Church, for example, is titled *Tenzi za Rohoni* (*Spiritual Poems*). The term *tenzi* refers to extended narrative poems of defined meter and rhyme, but none of the compositions in this collection meets this definition. Is the Swahili poetic terminology assuming different meanings based on religious differences?

Most other hymn collections are more appropriately defined by the term *nyimbo* (song)—such as the *Nyimbo Standard* (Standard Songs) of the Church Missionary Society, *Nyimbo za Injili* (Songs of the New Testament) of the Evangelical Church, *Nyimbo za Kikristo* (Christian Songs) of the Seventh-day Adventists, and *Nyimbo za Sifa* (Songs of Praise) of the Baptist church. In general, the *nyimbo* subgenre permits greater flexibility in rhyme and meter combinations than other Swahili poetic subgenres. Most of the verses that appear in these collections, in fact, have dispensed with conventional meter and rhyme altogether. A few others have used novel prosodic combinations in a way that does not seem to violate conventional Swahili prosodic formulas. In the four-line format, for example, which appears frequently in the collections, some of the most common combinations are the following:

a) A verse from the hymn "Who Can Wash Away . . .":

Verse	Meter	Rhyme
Hakuna kabisa	6	a
Dawa ya mokosa	6	a
Ya kututakasa	6	a
Ila damu yake, Yesu	8	b

There isn't anywhere
A cure for our sins

One that can cleanse us
Except the blood of Jesus

(Church Missionary Society 1969, 25; my translation)

b) A verse from the hymn "Only Trust Him."

Ni njia Yeye hakika	8	a
Hutuongoza rahani	8	b
Usikawe kumshika	8	a
Ili uwe barakani	8	b

It is His path for sure
That guides to eternal happiness
Don't delay in embracing Him
So that you can be blessed

(Church Missionary Society 1969, 47; my translation)

c) A verse from the hymn "Jesus Loves Me."

Anipenda kikweli	7	a
Mungu kanena hili	7	a
Sisi wake watoto	7	b
Kutulinda si zito	7	b

He truly loves me
God has said this
We are His children
Protecting us is not difficult (to Him)

This last verse demonstrates how the composers and translators of Swahili hymns attempted to draw from preexisting conventions of Swahili versification. For example, in the second line, it is the Swahili word *nena* from the Lamu dialect rather than the more common *sema* that is used for "say," reflecting the popular usage of Lamusims that was current in Swahili poetry of the time. In the third line, we witness a common poetic practice of word inversion—in this case *wake watoto* instead of the standard *watoto wake* for "his children"—in order to maintain a particular rhyme pattern.

Outside the format of four lines to a verse, there are other novel prosodic combinations, as in the following verse from the hymn "Come, for the Feast Is Spread":

Verse	Meter	Rhyme
Njoni karamuni	6	a
Mmeitwa	4	b
Vyakula mezani	6	a
Vimewekwa	4	b
Na mwake nyumbani	6	c
Mlazwe rahani	6	c
Mwake kifuani	6	c
Njooni, Njooni	6	d
Mkate wa kweli	6	a
Ametowa	4	b
Wa bure, si ghali	6	a
Utapewa	4	b
Wote awaita	6	c
Wengi wamepata	6	c
Nanyi awavuta	6	c
Njooni, Njooni	6	d

Come to the feast
    You have been summoned
The food is on the table
    Already spread
And in His home
You will rest happily
On His chest,
Come one, come all!

The real bread
    He has offered

Free of charge
   You shall be given
He is calling all
Many have (already) received
Now he is beckoning you
Come one, come all!

(Church Missionary Society 1969, 93; my translation)

But it is not only in the realm of poetry that Swahili literature began to develop an ecumenical legacy. Some writers have addressed Christian issues through imaginative prose, a genre that had no significant written record in Swahili literary history before the inception of European colonial rule. One of these is John Ndetei Sumba (1930–1970), a Kenyan novelist and, until his death in 1970, the editor of the Swahili Christian newspaper *Kesho* (Tomorrow). In his *Kuishi Kwingi ni Kuona Mengi* (Living Long Is Witnessing Much, 1968), Sumba subjects his main character, Katua, to much personal suffering for trying to prevent his wife, Kamene, from living a devout Christian life. As a consequence, Katua finally sees the light and becomes a practicing and upright Christian as he enters his old age. Another example is that of Serapius Komba (b. 1941), a Catholic friar of Tanzanian origin and a Swahili novelist, playwright, and poet of modest accomplishment. In Komba's *Pete* (The Ring, 1978), Tim ends up committing suicide in a church after violating his Christian vows and his expulsion from a seminary for succumbing to his obsession with virginity that leads him to marry a fifteen-year-old virgin. In K. W. Wamitila's *Nguvu za Sala* (The Power of Prayer, 1999), Richard, a devout Christian, struggles to ensure that his daughter Susan Ngunze embraces Christian values and does not succumb to the temptations of the material world. From the print pages of books and magazines to the screens and waves of the electronic media, therefore, a peculiarly Christian Swahili literature continues in verse as much as in drama and prose fiction.

When all is said and done, however, it is probably true that Christian-inspired literature in Swahili is still largely dependent on translations from English sources. This is evident in the translation of the gospels and hymns and in other texts on a wide range of themes, from intimate aspects of marital life to the existence of angels (based on the translation of Billy Graham's *Angels*, 1995) to how to run a business the Christian way. This raises the question of whether the full maturation of a Swahili Christianity must wait for a new generation of Christian-inspired writers ready to compose directly in Swahili. Or will the increasing secular concerns of Swahili writers across the religious divide eventually neutralize the ecumenical face of Swahili literature?

In 1962, Lyndon Harries suggested that even as the composition of Swahili poetry extended beyond the boundaries of ethnic Swahili, Islamic identity continued to be an important defining attribute of the composers.

> It is true that versification in Swahili is practiced today in roman script by many who cannot claim Swahili blood, but usually they are Muslims. Religion is the bond that gives them the right to share the medium of expression that has its origin in the Muslim religion. It is not religious verse that they write for the popular press, but the medium employed indicates familiarity with the Swahili way of life, which is fundamentally Islamic. (2)

But by the turn of the new century, that spirit of artistic sharing had gone not just beyond the boundaries of Swahili ethnicity but beyond the boundaries of Islamic identity. The literature had become truly multicultural in an ethnic as well as a religious sense.

If the Swahili language and Swahili literature came to serve Christian interests, however, they did not lose their Islamic appeal as far as the Swahili people were concerned. It has sometimes been suggested that culturally East African Islam (especially among the Swahili) has been more Arabized than West African Islam. Contrasting these two regions of Africa in their models of Islamization, Ali Mazrui has noted, for example, that

> in East Africa the Arab factor has been more pronounced in the arrival and expansion of Islam from the earliest days into the twen-

tieth century. Major religious leaders were overwhelmingly people who claimed Arab descent, if not indeed descent from the Prophet Muhammad himself. One adverse consequence of this Arab leadership was that it prolonged the image of Islam as a "foreign religion." (Mazrui 1995a, 262)

Ironically, however, rededication to the study of the Arabic language has been more a feature of the recent history of West African than of East African Islamic revivalism. Within East Africa, the Swahili language and Swahili literary production have been at the center of Islamic renewal in the twentieth and twenty-first centuries.

Until the beginning of the twentieth century, the pervasive role of Arabic in East African Islam was unchallenged. This was partly due to the status of the Qur'an in Muslim theology, which has no real equivalent in Christianity. The Qur'an is regarded not merely as divinely inspired but as literally the utterance of Allah, with the Prophet Muhammad serving as no more than a channel of communication. As a result, many believed that the translation of the Qur'an into Swahili was itself a sinful imitation of the Muslim Holy Book.

This view did not begin to change until the twentieth century under the influence of Sheikh Al-Amin bin Ali Mazrui, marking the beginning of a shift from Arabophile Islam to a Swahiliphile Islam, in spite of the central role that Arabic continued to play in Islamic ritual. Regarded as the leading Islamic reformer of the region in the first half of the twentieth century, Sheikh Al-Amin was a strong advocate of Arabic. He condemned as the height of religious ignorance the parroting of Qur'anic verses and passages in Arabic without any knowledge of their meaning. Appraising the central role of the Arabic language in the history of Islam generally and as the medium of the Qur'an and Islamic prayer, he regarded the study of Arabic as mandatory for every Muslim, male and female. If "the search for knowledge is mandatory for every Muslim man and Muslim woman," as the Prophet Muhammad is reported to have said, then that search needed to begin with the study of Arabic as a necessary tool for accessing the religious realm of human knowledge.

Nonetheless, Sheikh Al-Amin was quite instrumental in making Islamic knowledge accessible in Swahili. He pioneered the systematization of the Arabic script through the use of superscript and subscript diacritical symbols to make it more suitable for the writing of Swahili. (Hitherto different Swahili writers had used different letters of the Arabic alphabet to represent different uniquely Swahili sounds.) Sheikh Al-Amin also held regular classes on the translation and interpretation of the Qur'an; his work in mosque *madrassahs* eventually became the foundation for the Swahili translation of some Qur'anic *suras* undertaken posthumously in his name by Sheikh Muhammad Kasim Mazrui. Sheikh Al-Amin also translated some forty *hadiths* of the Prophet Muhammad; wrote on the Prophet Muhammad in Islamic, Jewish, and Christian scriptures; initiated an entirely new tradition of delivering portions of the sermon for Friday midday prayer in Swahili; and launched a Swahili newspaper devoted to Islamic affairs. In a real sense, then,

> As a scholar, Shaykh Al-Amin also attempted to be a bridge between Islam and modernity. He argued that while Christianity became the vanguard of progress when it became more secular and less Christian, Islam was the vanguard of progress when it was more Islamic and less secular. Accord to Al-amin, progress among Muslims required not the abandonment of Islam but the recovery of the original spirit of Islamic enlightenment (Yusuf 2005, 2)

His advocacy of both Arabic and Swahili in East African Islam was partly a product of this wider commitment to promoting an "alternative modernity" rooted in Islam.

Sheikh Al-Amin's legacy was later inherited and nurtured by some of his disciples, especially Sheikh Muhammad Kasim Mazrui and Sheikh Abdallah Saleh Farsy, who served consecutively as chief *khadis* of Kenya. The two sternly opposed the dogmatic position that came especially from the ranks of the *shariifs* of East Africa—those who claim a blood relationship with the Prophet Muhammad—that insisted on an Arabic Islam everywhere and at whatever cost. By producing published translations of the Qur'an in Swahili and making the language the primary medium of their religious presentations and publications—from Islamic theology to Islamic poetry—the two, with others of their generation, made a significant contribution to the consolidation of the place of Swahili as the language of East African Islam.

Islamic resurgence in the 1980s and 1990s gave a further boost to the language, as young and fiery Muslim preachers from Mombasa to Zanzibar turned to it as an instrument of an intellectual jihad. Some of the disciples of Sheikh Muhammad Kasim Mazrui and Sheikh Abdallah Saleh Farsy continued to expand its role in East African Islam. Sheikh Abdallah's ideas, for example, "are being continued today by his pupils, notable among whom is Sheikh Saidi Musa (b. 1944), who writes extensively from his headquarters at Ugwene, Moshi, on mainland Tanzania. The outcome is that Swahili has today made inroads in areas previously reserved for Arabic" (Topan 1997, 917).

In the meantime, the momentum of Sheikh Muhammad Kasim Mazrui's efforts to recenter Swahili as the language of Islamic identity did not build up until well after his death in 1982. The demand for English in Mombasa—because of results indicating that women perform better in that language than men do in school exams—once led Sheikh Muhammad Kasim Mazrui to warn against the dangers of English in his Swahili periodical, *Sauti ya Haki*. In his words:

> Hatuna budi kukisoma na kukijua Kizungu, kwani Kizungu leo ndiyo lugha ya maishilio. Lakini yataka tusisahau kuwa kuna ulimwengu mkubwa zaidi wa dini na mila zetu. Tusipojitahadhari Kizungu kitatumiza wazimwazima—hata fikra zetu ziwe ni za kizungu. Hatari hii ya Kizungu ni lazima itiliwe seng'enge na busara ipatikanayo katika Kiarabu na Kiswahili. Ni muhimu basi vyuo vyetu visiwe ni venye kufundisha kusoma Qur'ani peke yake; lakini tuvitumie pia kufundishia mantiki itokanayo na Uislamu na

ilmu za kidunia kwa lugha zetu wenyewe: Kiswahili na Kiarabu. Na jukumu hili ni kubwa zaidi kwa wanawake, kwani wao ndio walezi wakubwa wa watoto wetu majumbani.

We have no alternative but to study and know English, because today English is the language of livelihood. But we must not forget that there is also the larger world of religion and our traditions. If we are not careful the English language will swallow us completely—even our thoughts will now be cast in an English mode. The danger of English must be tempered by the wisdom encapsulated in both Arabic and Kiswahili. It is therefore imperative that our Qur'anic schools offer learning not only in Qur'anic literacy but are also used to teach the logic arising from Islam as well as secular subjects in our own languages, Swahili and Arabic. And this responsibility [of acquiring this integrated knowledge] is greater for women, for it is they who do much of the parenting in our homes. (*Sauti ya Haki*, August 1972; my translation)

Sheikh Muhammad Kasim Mazrui's relativistic thinking is clear: English is a carrier of western values and its cognitive effects can be counteracted only by concerted efforts to recenter languages such as Swahili and Arabic, which he regards as the custodians of Afro-Islamic values and traditions. Though Arabic is not widely spoken in the community, it has a special place in the world of Islam as a language of religious ritual and doctrinal revelation.

In his continued advocacy for the introduction of secular subjects in religious schools within an Afro-Islamic epistemology, Sheikh Muhammad Kasim Mazrui shatters the boundaries between the religious and the secular. He argues that "karibu elimu zote zinazojulikana kama 'elimu za kidunia' zingelifaa ziitwe 'elimu za dini' pia, kwa sababu ya uhusiano wake na dini, na kwa kuwa elimu hizo zahitajika katika [kuifahamu] dini" (virtually all the subjects that constitute "secular education" should also be regarded as "religious education" because of their interrelationship with religion and because those subjects are needed in understanding religion [better]); *Sauti ya Haki*, November 1972; my translation). He elaborates that those who know something about the laws of physics, the equations of chemistry, and the processes of biology are generally better placed to appreciate the creative genius of the Almighty Allah as inscribed in the Holy Qur'an than those who lack such knowledge. What is not clear is the extent to which Sheikh Muhammad Kasim's views were inspired by the example of Al-Azhar University in Cairo, an institution that began over a thousand years ago as an Islamic center of higher learning but later introduced a parallel secular curriculum.

It was almost two decades before Sheikh Muhammad Kasim's call began to be embraced and given institutional validation, beginning perhaps with the establishment of the Madrassah Resource Center (MRC) in Mombasa in 1988. As we know, successive postcolonial African governments in Kenya have been introducing English earlier in the educational pyramid than the British colonizers themselves did. In major towns such as Nairobi, Mombasa, Kisumu, and Nakuru, the exercise begins as early as the kindergarten. For some observers in the local community, an emphasis on English-medium learning from the earliest years of a child's education is an invasion of the minds of the young that inflicts irreparable damage on their epistemological orientation. As a result, community demands grew for an alternative education, demands that, at the level of early child education, finally crystallized in the form of the Madrassah Resource Center.

Established as a service nongovernmental organization, the MRC represents a creative effort to build on the local "traditional" educational institutions, the *madrassah,* while developing them in tandem with national goals. Hitherto exclusively devoted to religious education, the scores of participating *madrassahs* began to introduce complementary secular material and activities under the coordination of the MRC. The approach the MRC advocates emphasizes "the use of low-cost, locally available indigenous material and promotes activities that integrate local motifs and narratives from oral as well as written traditions. These components ensure that education is economically, socially and culturally accessible and appropriate" (Aga Khan Foundation 1998, 4).

Central to the logic of the entire project is instruction in Swahili as the Arabic language is introduced in small, incremental amounts. According to the MRC's founder-director, Swafiya Muhashamy, the focus on Swahili is crucial because the curriculum and approach are designed to meet parental expectations that the children will be socialized into the fundamentals of the cultural thought of the community (MRC annual report, February 1993).

In all these efforts, the MRC is not seeking to deny the children the opportunity to acquire English. Rather, the objective is to have the children more solidly grounded in the epistemological tradition of their community before proceeding to be exposed to "the other world." With the kind of foundation provided by this alternative early education, followed by a similar alternative paradigm of training at the higher levels, the expectation is that the children will have been armed with skills that will enable them test what they "receive" in the national school system against the value of what is "intrinsic" in their own linguistic worldview.

Another example of this trend is the community-based and community-sponsored Ma'ahad Nuur in Mombasa, an Islamic *madrassah* that provides instruction in a wide range of Islamic subjects as well as the Arabic language, with Swahili as the medium of instruction. Founded as a school for Swahili female youth, it now attracts many older women who study side by side with the youth. Similar, some less formal, community learning initiatives have sprung up throughout the Kenya coast, in which women have been the galvanizing force. With this newly acquired Islamic understanding, these "mothers" hope to turn the domestic space into a more successful arena for combating what they see as unchecked westernization. In the process, Swahili has acquired a new role as a language of Islamicist counterhegemonic discourse.

These examples from the Afro-Islamic community of Mombasa seem to vindicate Anthony Giddens's assertion that globalization

> is not just an "out there" phenomenon, referring solely to the emergence of large scale world systems. . . . [It also refers to]

transformations in [the] texture of everyday life. It is an "in here" phenomenon, affecting even intimacies of personal identities. . . . Globalization invades local contexts of action but does not destroy them; on the contrary, new forms of local cultural identity and self-expression, are causally bound up with globalizing processes. (1996, 367–38)

But as Alidou (2005) and others have amply demonstrated, where local contexts are not destroyed by forces of globalization, it is often the result of specific, community-based acts of resistance against certain effects of globalization. The examples provided here are further evidence of how "resistance" to globalization in the linguistic domain has prevented the elimination of local identities by reshaping them in response to new challenges. And in this transformation, they too came to symbolize that complex world of the glocal—a kind of unique local articulation of the global.

But why did these educational acts of resistance come to life when they did, nearly two decades after Sheikh Muhammad Kasim Mazrui made his call for alternative schools? Part of the answer lies in post–Cold War global politics in the context of the reemergence of the politics of pluralism in the local landscape. They were triggered in part by popular perceptions that the West in general and the United States in particular have increasingly assumed a posture that is decidedly anti-Islamic. Their views are not unlike those of John E. Woods, a professor of Middle Eastern history at the University of Chicago, who made the observation that "almost immediately after the collapse of Communism, Islam emerged as the new evil force" in the imagination of the American government (*New York Times*, August 28, 1995). Recent pressures of the U.S. government on the government of Kenya to enact anti-terrorist legislation (which is seen by many as anti-Muslim) and other local factors have added fuel to local fears of negative "othering" on the grounds of Islamic identity. These developments seem to have consolidated the resolve of the Afro-Islamic constituency in the country to promote an alternative education that would give fresh momentum not only to their

Afro Islamic identity but also to an Afro-Islamocentric view of the world, for better or for worse. In other words, the particular manner in which the global is signified locally may ultimately depend on the specific (economic, political, social) conjuncture of forces of both global and local origins.

The resurgence of political Islam, both globally and locally (within the Swahili-speaking regions of East Africa), also stimulated the production of three additional Swahili translations of the Qur'an. There is, first, the *Tarjama ya Al-Muntakhab* by Ali Muhsin al-Barwani, who was minister of education in Zanzibar before the 1964 revolution. The translation is based on the Arabic interpretation of the Qur'an authenticated by the Committee on the Qur'an and Sunnah of the Egyptian Supreme Council of Islamic Affairs. A particularly prominent aspect of al-Barwani's translation is the influence of his linguistic nationalism, which seeks to reinscribe a Swahili of the native speakers of Zanzibar. He argues in his preface to the translation:

> Mtaona mimi humu sikutumia maandishi yangu kwa mujibu wa mtindo unaojulikana kama ni wa "Standard Swahili." Mimi nimejitahidi kuandika kama ninavyo sema mimi mwenyewe, au kama nilivyo kuwa nawasikia wazazi wangu wakisema nami. Wao na wenzao wao nawachukulia kama ni mfano mwema wa kusema Kiswahili kwa kuwa hawakuharibiwa lugha yao kwa maskuli tulio pelekwa sisi.

> You will see that in here I did not render my work in accordance with the style known as "Standard Swahili." I have endeavored to write as I myself normally speak, or as I heard my parents speaking to me. I take them and their generation as a good example of spoken Swahili, for their language was not contaminated by the kind of schools we were sent to. (1995, vii; my translation)

Here al-Barwani betrays the same anti–Standard Swahili sentiments as Sheikh Al-Amin bin Ali Mazrui, seeing it as a linguistic corruption rooted in the Euro-Christian colonial legacy. And if Sheikh Al-Amin's objections to Standard Swahili were targeted at the phonological level, al-Barwani's objections extend to the level of word structure, contending that Swahili relative clauses such as *aliyekuja* (the person who came) should be written not as one word (as is the practice in Standard Swahili) but as two words, as was the practice in the Swahili *ajami* tradition.

In the same preface, al-Barwani advocates a two-pronged strategy to counteract the negative effects of Standard Swahili. One is a total reform of the roman script to bring it to greater conformity with the pronunciation patterns of the Swahili people. The other is the "revival" of *ajami* literacy,

> kufundisha watu kutumia harufi za Kiarabu kuandikia Kiswahili kama walivyo kuwa wakiandika wote hapo zamani kabla ya kuja wakoloni. Hapana jambo jepesi kama hilo. Kwa majaribio yangu nimeweza kuwafundisha vijana kadhaa wa Kitanzania kusoma na kuandika kwa harufi za Kiarabu kwa muda wa siku chache tu na wakaweza kusoma Qur'an popote nilipowafungulia.

teaching people to use the Arabic alphabet in writing Swahili as all the people in the past used to write before the arrival of colonialists. There is nothing simpler than that. In my own experimentation I was able to instruct several Tanzanian youth to read and write using the Arabic alphabet in a matter of a few days and they were able to read the Qur'an on any page I opened for them. (1995, vii; my translation)

Al-Barwani seems to be advocating the use of the *ajami* script not only to promote literacy in Swahili but also as a transitional strategy toward Qur'anic literacy. Whatever the case, what began as a religious exercise in Qur'anic translation became intertwined with a project in linguistic nationalism.

The second recent Swahili translation of the Qur'an is the *Tafsir Al-Kashif* of Sheikh Hassan Ali Mwalupa. This translation is still in process; it is being released in several volumes, chapter by chapter. By March 2006, ten volumes had been published. Mwalupa's translation is based on the Arabic original of the Lebanese scholar Sheikh Muhammad Jawad Mughniyya, and this may be the first Shi'a-inspired Swahili translation of the Qur'an. What Mwalupa finds particularly attractive in Mughniyya's work is its targeted audience: the young modern generation that has been captured by such western ideologies as capitalism, socialism, and democracy. To the translator, Tanzanian Muslim youth were in need of precisely such a translation as they confronted national marginalization and global hostility because of their religious identity.

In the preface to his rendering of the Qur'an, Mughniyya proposes a theory of Qur'anic translation, the main thrust of which is that it is not enough for the translator to be versed in the Arabic language and the various disciplines of the Islamic sciences. The translator must do more than understand the divine revelation: (s)he must actually "feel" its essence in all its dimensions in his/her very "heart." The faith of the translator in the message of the Qur'an must flow in his/her very flesh and blood (2003, xvi).

These two Swahili translations share two common attributes. First, unlike the translations of their predecessors, which included lengthy remarks of the translators, these two confine themselves to reproducing in Swahili the Arabic translations and commentaries of the Qur'an undertaken by other scholars with minimal inscription of their own thoughts and ideas. Second, both attempt to maintain a certain degree of neutrality in critical areas of difference between the various Islamic denominations and schools of thought. With regard to this latter point, the translators hope to promote a sense of unity among East African Muslims at a time when the *ummah* is under attack by American-led forces of post–Cold War globalization.

The publication of al-Barwani's translation coincided with the production of yet another Swahili translation of the Qur'an— Sheikh Said Moosa Mohamed al-Kindy's *Asili ya Uongofu Katika Uhakika wa Materemsho na Ubainisho wa Tafsiri* (Source of Guidance in the Original Revelation and As Clarified in Translation, 1995). Like Mwalupa's translation, this is a work in progress and is being released in installments: ten volumes had been published by March 2006. But unlike Mwalupa's and al-Barwani's translations, al-Kindy's follows in the tradition of Sheikh Al-Amin bin Ali Mazrui and Sheikh Abdallah Saleh Farsy; he provides his own elaborate commentaries synthesized from a variety of sources.

These new translations reflect the new political tensions in the East African region as well as globally; Muslim communities feel that they are being marginalized and their religion demonized. Making the Qur'an available in Swahili becomes a means for them to gain a better understanding of their religion and galvanize their collective consciousness for purposes of counteracting the generalized state of hostility, but it also becomes a symbol that contributes to the consolidation of their sense of belonging in Islam.

This era is also marked by a rebirth of Islamic newspapers in Swahili, reviving a trend first initiated by Sheikh Al-Amin in the early 1930s. Swahili-language newspapers such as *An-Najah* and *Sharafa la Mwislamu* routinely carry special columns of poetry on topical issues of the moment. They publish not only letters but also poems to the editor on a wide range of subjects such as inflation, debt, and government policy. A similar tradition has now established itself in Swahili Islamic periodicals, providing space for Swahili poetry that calls on the Muslim *ummah* to hold fast to the uniting and guiding rope of Allah and advocates Islamic conduct in the collective and individual lives of the believers. More influential still have been the programs of Radio Rahma in Mombasa, a Muslim-controlled radio station that uses Swahili as its primary medium of communication. Swahili religious songs and poetry constitute an important part of the religious menu of the radio station. As Swahili ceases to be an Islamic language at the national and regional level, is it reclaiming its Islamicity at the more local, ethnic level of the Swahili?

In the final analysis, the contradictions of Africa's triple heritage—indigenous, Islamic, and Euro-Christian—continue to condition the interplay between language, literature, and religious faith in the stark realities of postcolonial history. The story of the Swahili language and its literature is one of both tension and accommodation between Islam, Christianity, and more indigenous religious traditions of Africa. But even as the language and its literary products expand their ecumenical horizons, in the process becoming increasingly diversified along religious lines, their Afro-Islamic core continues to demonstrate remarkable resilience, constantly feeding the Afro-Islamic identity of the native speakers of the East African lingua franca, Swahili. Where the religion had once Islamized the Swahili language and culture, the language is now gradually Swahilizing Islam, seeking to give it more of an indigenous imprint.

4

Translation and the (Re)Configuration of the Swahili Literary Space

Contrary to the focus of translation studies in the West on the re-lationship between the translated text and the original text, the most pressing issue in Swahiliphone Africa has been about the re-lationship of the translated text to the literature of its translating language. In the theoretical terrain, translated texts have often been regarded as part of the literary corpus of the original (as when we speak of Russian literature in English translation, for example). More recently, some have argued that the translated text is relatively autonomous from its source text. The 1980s, in fact, are said to have opened with a good deal of agreement be-tween various theoretical models (including semiotics, discourse analysis, and poststructuralist textual theory) "that translation is an independent form of writing, distinct from the foreign text and from texts originally written in the translating language. Trans-lating is seen as enacting its own processes of signification which answer to different linguistic and cultural contexts" (Venuti 2000, 215). But in assuming a life of its own, can a translated text even-tually also acquire a literary identity of its translating language? This certainly seems to have been the orientation in East Africa with regard to some texts translated into Swahili. In this chapter, I analyze this literary development in relation to translations into

Swahili of some of Shakespeare's plays and George Orwell's *Animal Farm*.

The Swahili language has had a long history of accommodating translated works, initially from the East and later from the West and other parts of Africa. According to available evidence, the first major translation into Swahili and the one that remains most widely known from the precolonial period is the *Hamziyya*, which is based on an Arabic poem on the life of the Prophet Muhammad. The Swahili of the translated text is said to be "so archaic that it can not be dated later than the 17th century, although the earliest extant manuscript is dated 1784" (Knappert 1967, 3). But the proliferation of translated works in Swahili did not take place until after the inception of European colonial rule in Africa, toward the end of the nineteenth century.

Swahili translations of English-language texts can be divided into three phases. The earliest, which appeared in the early colonial period, were primarily—though not exclusively—translation of portions of the Bible. According to Jack T. Rollins, during the early part of European-Swahili contact there was an outpouring of biblical material in Swahili produced especially by missionaries (1983, 62). Invariably, these were intended for evangelical purposes as Christianity tried to make inroads into the East African region. In this same period, Christian missionaries translated Bunyan's *Pilgrim's Progress*, *Aesop's Tales*, and a few other literary works.

The second phase spans the late 1920s to the early 1940s, when an influx of Swahili translations of English classics was done by British colonial education officers and some missionaries. This period coincided with increasing interest among members of the British colonial establishment in standardizing Swahili, using it as a medium of instruction in lower elementary education in some regions of their dominion, and teaching it as a subject in the upper levels. These translations, it appears, were intended to fill a gap in Swahili readers for schools and perhaps provide models that would encourage East African nationals to write prose fiction along similar lines. Texts translated during this phase included Robert Louis Stevenson's *Treasure Island*, Rudyard Kipling's

Mowgli Stories, Jonathan Swift's *Gulliver's Travels*, Rider Haggard's *Allan Quatermain* and *King Solomon's Mines*, and Lewis Carroll's *Alice in Wonderland.*

Of particular note during this period is the 1935 serialized and abridged translation of Booker T. Washington's *Up from Slavery* under the title *Mtu Mweusi Mtukufu* (The Honorable Black Man) by a leading British colonial educational administrator, G. B. Johnson. The series appeared in the popular periodical *Mazungumzo ya Walimu wa Unguja* (Conversation among Teachers of Zanzibar), whose purpose was to foster dialogue among those working within the colonial educational establishment. As Ousseina Alidou explains, the publication of this text coincided with the colonial establishment of a vocational school for African students in the East African island of Zanzibar, which was then under British rule (Alidou 2000). The Swahili version of the life of Booker T. Washington was seemingly intended to provide legitimacy for this new vocational orientation of colonial education as one that was supposedly more compatible with the condition of Black people in the colonies.[1]

It is not until the early postcolonial period of the 1960s that we begin to see the third wave of Swahili literary translations, which involved not just English classics but other European works available in English as well. Some of these are clearly translations of translations. The Swahili translations of William Shakespeare's *Julius Caesar* and *Merchant of Venice*, Nikolai Gogol's *Government Inspector*, Maxim Gorky's *Mother*, Bertolt Brecht's *Good Woman of Setzuan*, and George Orwell's *Animal Farm* were all products of this period. So were the translations of works in English by African authors such as Chinua Achebe's *No Longer at Ease*, Ayi Kwei Armah's *The Beautiful Ones Are Not Yet Born*, Peter Abraham's *Mine Boy*, and Wole Soyinka's *The Trials of Brother Jero.*

In 1993, Macmillan (Kenya) Publishers released a number of Swahili translations from its 1958 "Stories to Remember" series. These include *Ngano za Ajabu Kutoka Ugiriki* (*Wonder Tales from Greece*, translated by Abdi Sultani), *Robinson Crusoe Kisiwani*

(*Robinson Crusoe*, by Daniel Defoe), *Safari za Gulliver* (*Gulliver's Travels*, by Jonathan Swift), *Kisiwa cha Matumbawe* (*Coral Island*, by R. M. Ballantyne), *Visa vya Oliver Twist* (*Oliver Twist*, by Charles Dickens), *Visa vya David Copperfield* (*David Copperfield*, also by Dickens), *Kisiwa Chenye Hazina* (*Treasure Island*, by Robert Louis Stevenson), *Kuzunguka Dunia kwa Siku Themanini* (*Around the World in Eighty Days*, by Jules Verne), and *Hekaya za Miujiza Arabuni* (*Strange Tales from the Arabian Nights*, as narrated by Margery Green). Typical of the translated works of this (post-colonial) period, these narratives were all rendered into Swahili by East Africans. This Macmillan project was partly inspired by the hope that its translated texts might some day be adopted in the national Swahili-literature syllabus.

These translations vary widely in terms of their artistic quality and presumed fidelity to the "original." On the one extreme, we have rather liberal translations like that of Lewis Carroll's *Alice in Wonderland*, so liberal, in fact, that it led one observer, Lyndon Harries, to make the following remarks:

> The translator presents Alice as a Swahili-speaking African girl! A Swahili-speaking Alice is a charming idea, something that I feel sure Lewis Carroll would have been happy to discover, but by making this transformation surely the translator has done more than a translator has a right to do. His desire to appeal to his African audience has taken him much too far. By presenting Alice as an African girl he makes it impossible for him to remain objective and consequently faithful to his text. (1970, 30)

Along similar lines, S. S. Mushi reminds us in the introduction of his Swahili translation of Shakespeare's *Macbeth* that his work was guided less by the imperative of fidelity to the original than by sensitivity to the Swahili lingocultural milieu of the audience (1968, vi–vii).

On the other extreme of the fidelity spectrum are translations that have ostensibly attempted to be as "faithful" to the original texts as possible. Julius Nyerere's translations of Shakespeare's work, for example, were clearly informed by the idea that the best translation is the one that is closest to the original in form, meaning, and style. Like Spivak, perhaps, he seems to have believed in fidelity to the original in principle "not because it is possible, but because one must try" (Spivak 2001, 14). Nyerere even proceeded to produce a revised edition of his translation of *Julius Caesar* to eliminate certain errors he had supposedly committed in the first edition (1969, vi) in a conscious attempt to bring it into closer conformity with the original.

Some of these translated texts eventually came to be included in the very definition of Swahili literature. It is up to the "subaltern" to make a conscious decision to define the status of the product in relation to her/his literary space—and sometimes she or he domesticates and absorbs it into the target corpus of literary texts. What, then, are the circumstances that may have led to the absorption of translations of Shakespeare's plays and *Shamba la Wanyama*, the Swahili translation of Orwell's *Animal Farm*, for example, into the body of Swahili literature courses? It is to this question that we shall now turn.

Shakespeare is widely regarded not only as the greatest writer in the English language but also as the greatest writer in any language in human history. A school of thought has emerged in the West, however, that has questioned the continued prominence and centrality of Shakespeare in the western literary canon. According to Harold Bloom, there are "resenters" who have been attempting to scatter Shakespeare with the aim of undoing the canon by dissolving its very center. This "School of Resentment," argues Bloom,

> is compelled by its dogmas to regard aesthetic supremacy, particularly in Shakespeare's instance, as a prolonged cultural conspiracy undertaken to protect the political and economic interests of mercantile Great Britain from the eighteenth century until today. In contemporary America, the polemic shifts to a Shakespeare utilized as a Eurocentric center of power in order to oppose the legitimate cultural aspirations of various minorities,

including academic Feminists, who are now scarcely a minority. (1994, 53)

While Bloom is right that feminists are more visible in the American academy than they were twenty years ago, his suggestion that they are now "scarcely a minority" is altogether wrong. But whatever may be Bloom's position on the matter, there is little doubt that the place of Shakespeare in the canon has been under interrogation in western scholarship.

As Shakespeare was coming under attack in the West, however, Daniel Arap Moi, then the president of Kenya, defended him not only in terms of his place in the western canon but also more generally in terms of his universal importance as a literary figure. In a public address on July 25, 1989, President Moi paid tribute to Shakespeare as a literary genius of universal acclaim and directed that his works be accorded a permanent place in the country's literature curriculum and education (*Daily Nation* [Nairobi], July 26, 1989).

President Moi was apparently reacting to a particular school of cultural nationalists whose objectives included the total "Africanization" of the high school literature curriculum in Kenya. By 1985, Shakespeare was the only non-African artist in the English-language literature syllabus for high schools who had not fallen under the cloud of rejection. But the nationalist push for reculturation—for the attempted recovery of areas of authenticity that had been lost in the process of western acculturation—eventually managed to rid the Kenya literature syllabus of even this last bastion of English literature. It took the presidential intervention of Daniel Arap Moi to restore Shakespeare, beginning with *Romeo and Juliet* as one of the set texts for the 1992 national high school literature examination.

President Moi was not, of course, in the same intellectual league as the Nyereres, Senghors, and Nkrumahs of Africa, philosopher-kings who could read Shakespeare and appreciate his genius. He was not a literary intellectual in the sense used by Ali Mazrui as "a person who is engaged in a serious way in literary activity, and who is fascinated by literary ideas" (1975, 103–4). One therefore has to understand Moi's claim that his directive to reintroduce Shakespeare was due to his personal appreciation of the man's genius as only part of the story.

Nor could Moi be regarded as a universalist who was inclined to assess the worth of culture and its products in terms that are not bound by nation or ethnicity. It is true, of course, that in his own book, *Kenya African Nationalism: Nyayo Philosophy and Principles,* Moi advocates a kind of nationalism that accommodates external influences, especially those from the West. Unlike his predecessor, Jomo Kenyatta, for example, Moi explicitly embraced a western-introduced Christianity as one of the important cornerstones of his nationalist ideology. But Moi's record as president of Kenya from 1978 to 2002 suggests that his openness to the West may have had less to do with a maturing of his nationalism than with a dependency syndrome that has bedeviled African leadership over the decades. Could this dependency factor, then, better explain Moi's intervention on behalf of Shakespeare? Could the British government, for example, which had been investing substantial amounts of funds in Kenya's educational system, especially in the teaching of English language and literatures (see Mazrui and Mazrui 1998, 147–49), have influenced the president to rehabilitate Shakespeare in Kenyan schools? These questions may remain unanswered for the time being.

What is certain in this entire saga is that the cultural nationalism that threatened the place of Shakespeare in Kenya was itself a reaction to conditions precipitated by colonialism. At the dawn of independence it was felt that the literature-in-English syllabus had been too Eurocentric, emphasizing as it did the study of European at the expense of African authors. The literature syllabus needed to be "Africanized." In the area of drama, in particular, Ngugi wa Thiong'o traces the beginnings of an anti-Shakespearean revolt in Kenya to the 1950s when the anticolonial struggle was at its peak (1986b, 39). But nationalistic sentiments about the English-language literature syllabus in general did not openly manifest themselves until the postcolonial period.

These nationalistic feelings were initially expressed by African academics at the University of Nairobi. In response to the apparent Eurocentric bias of the English Department curriculum, some lecturers issued a statement in October 1968 with the following declaration:

> We reject the primacy of English literature and culture. The aim, in short, should be to orient ourselves towards PLACING Kenya, East Africa and then Africa at the center. All other things are to be considered in their relevance to our situation and their contribution towards understanding ourselves. (Quoted in Ngugi 1986b, 94)

These views found immediate support from other African academics at the university, and when they became the subject of newspaper debates, they seemed to reflect the popular will of a large section of the Kenyan community. The views were later also endorsed by academics from other universities in the region who participated at the 1969 Nairobi Conference of English and Literature Departments of the Universities of East and Central Africa (Ngugi 1986b, 95). As a result of these initiatives, the literature syllabus of the University of Nairobi began to take a more Africa-centered and world-centered turn.

The cultural nationalist momentum that began at the university level soon extended to the country's secondary schools. Several university academics were determined to pressure the government to Africanize the English-language literature syllabus for secondary education. Their efforts ultimately led to the 1974 Nairobi conference on the teaching of African literature in Kenyan schools. Though thematically focusing on Kenya, this conference too was international in the scope of its presenters and audience; participants came from Kenya, Uganda, Tanzania, and Malawi. The Kenyan participants noted with dismay that

> even ten years after Independence, in practically every school in the republic our students were being subjected to alien cultural values which are meaningless especially to our present needs. Al-

most all books used in our schools are written by foreign authors; out of 57 texts of drama studied at EAACE [East African Advanced Certificate of Education] level in our schools between 1968 and 1972 only one was African. (Quoted in Ngugi 1986b, 100)

At the end of the conference, participants were virtually unanimous in calling for a rapid move toward a more Africa-centered syllabus for secondary schools.

As university academics became increasingly involved in designing high school examinations and curricula and as more university graduates who had been influenced by the nationalist school of thought found employment in secondary education policy bodies such as the Kenya Institute of Education, Kenya's Ministry of Higher Education, and the Kenya Examinations Council, the English-language literature syllabus was gradually transformed to become more African in focus. This partly led to the exclusion of non-African authors, except for Shakespeare. But then, as Ali Mazrui asked, "Did the reputation of Shakespeare among Africans [now] have to go through the second phase of African cultural nationalism—the phase of being rejected as non-African?" (1967b, 109). Yes, in Kenya at least, in the nationalist zeal to pursue the Africanization agenda to its ultimate end, Shakespeare too lost his place altogether in Kenyan schools by 1985 until he was rehabilitated by President Daniel Arap Moi in 1992.

Ironically, however, the attempted elimination of Shakespeare from the study of literature in the language in which the man himself spoke and composed stands in marked contrast to his seemingly more secure place in Swahili-language literature. As Shakespeare in English was being purged from the English-language literature syllabus, Shakespeare in Swahili was being embraced as part of Kenya's Swahili-literature syllabus for upper secondary schools and in universities.

As indicated earlier, in certain European critical and pedagogical practices, translations are often treated as the expression of "the other," suitable for a study of the literature of "the other," especially in comparative literature courses and writings. Within this western view, both Wole Soyinka's *Lion and the Jewel* and Bertolt Brecht's *The Good Woman of Setzuan*, for example, would be considered expressions of literature in English, but in differ- ent senses. Soyinka's play was originally composed in English, while Brecht's play is an English translation of a German origi- nal and would normally be treated as a work of German litera- ture in English translation. It is conceivable that Soyinka's play could one day be included in the *Norton Anthology of English Lit- erature*, while Brecht's play stands little chance of appearing in such a collection. The sixth edition of the anthology includes, for example, the works of South African novelist Nadine Gordimer to reflect "even more the international nature of literature in En- glish" (Abrams 1993, xxxi). Of course, Gordimer is a South Afri- can writer of European ancestry. But a time may come when non- European writers in the English language will be appropriately accommodated. Whatever the case, the western position appears to contrast with the Swahili position on translated works.

Coming from this European perspective, Lyndon Harries had once hoped that Swahili translations of European and other clas- sics would one day constitute useful material for a course on litera- ture in translation in Tanzania. Translations of European clas- sics into Swahili reminded Harries "that in many universities there are courses on Literature in Translation." Similar courses, he sug- gested, could be designed and made part of the educational process in Tanzania and presumably in other Swahili-speaking areas of Africa (1970, 31). In Kenya, at least, the situation developed fur- ther than Harries had hoped. Some of the translated works actu- ally came to be regarded not as literature in translation but as part of literature in Swahili. And it is perhaps in conformity with this general sentiment with regard to literary translation that Ezekiel Kazungu (1984), Sheila Ryanga (1985), Alamin Mazrui (1981b), and Mwenda Ntarangwi (2004) all came to include trans- lated texts in their definitions of Swahili-language literature. And some of those texts were indeed those of Shakespeare.

The first Swahili exposure to Shakespeare was in prose. This appeared in a collection entitled *Hadithi Ingereza* (English Tales), produced by the Universities Mission to Central Africa in Zanzibar in 1900. The collection contains Swahili prose renderings of *The Taming of the Shrew* (translated as *Mwanamke Aliyefugwa*), *The Merchant of Venice* (translated as *Kuwia na Kuwiwa*), *The Tragedy of King Lear* (translated as *Baba na Binti*), and *The Life of Timon of Athens* (translated as *Kula Maji*). Jack D. Rollins mentions an earlier Swahili collection of Shakespearean tales based on Charles and Mary Lamb's *Tales from Shakespeare* that was translated by Bishop Steere and appeared in 1867 (1983, 62). What is particularly striking about this collection of translated texts is the extent to which it tried to be sensitive to the Swahili cultural universe. The anonymous translator—who most likely was of European origin—attempted to breathe Swahili life and culture into the translation, resulting in an independent interpretation of Shakespeare.

The first Swahili translations of some of Shakespeare's plays as plays, however, are those of Mwalimu Julius K. Nyerere, the first president of the Republic of Tanzania. When cultural nationalist sentiments in Africa were still at their peak, Julius Nyerere translated both *Julius Caesar* (1963, 1969) and *The Merchant of Venice* (1972), texts to which he was exposed when he was a student at Edinburgh University. S. S. Mushi's translation of Shakespeare's *Macbeth* (1968) was also done during this time period.

In the introduction to his translation, Mushi makes it clear that he did not intend to be faithful to the original; rather, his objective was to reproduce the message of Shakespeare. The Swahili saying "Kikulacho ki nguoni mwako" ("That which stings you is in your own clothes") is considered a better rendering of the line from Shakespeare's Macbeth "The near in blood, the nearer bloody" than a more literal translation in Swahili which would sound virtually meaningless to the speakers of the language. Nyerere, on the other hand, seemed less conscious about "Swahilizing" his translation, in its first edition, of *Julius Caesar*. It was, as it were, a translation undertaken by Nyerere for Nyerere without regard to an audience "out there." As he indicates in his introduction, he engaged in the task of translating *Julius Caesar* without intending to have the final product published (1963, 3). It was in the revised edition, after Nyerere had more decisively moved to the left, that he tried to be more conscious about Swahilizing his translation. For example, virtually all the names of the characters in the first edition were more or less the same as those in the English original. In the revised edition, however, these were all phonetically Swahilized. Even the title changed from *Julius Caezar* to *Juliasi Kaizari.*

One of the factors that inspired Nyerere to Swahilize his revised edition, of course, had to do with poetic quality. In their translations, both Nyerere and Mushi tried to retain the blank verse style of the original. But since Swahili is an open-syllable language while English is not, Nyerere was constantly forced into a balancing act between a Swahili and English metric system. The names as they appeared in the original posed a particularly daunting metric problem for those who did not understand English at all. What would be the number of "Swahili meter" for names like "Caesar" or "Brutus"? But by Swahilizing them to "Siza" and "Buruto" the subconscious problem of metric beat would be resolved for Swahili-speaking readers. For Nyerere, these metric concerns were also important because they would conform better to the "African practice" of singing rather than merely reading verse. They would heighten the "singability" of the blank verse sections of the play.

The Swahili translations of Shakespeare that have appeared repeatedly in the Kenya high school Swahili-literature syllabus are those of Nyerere, namely *Juliasi Kaizari* (*Julius Caesar*) and *Mapebari wa Venisi* (*The Merchant of Venice*). Mushi's *Makbeth* has not been as successful in the educational arena, perhaps because of where the work was originally published. Unlike Nyerere's translations, which were published in Kenya by Oxford University Press, *Makbeth* was published in Tanzania by Tanzania Publishing House. Mushi's translation, therefore, was less accessible in Kenya than Nyerere's, especially for the years when relations between the two East African countries were strained. Kenyan students, therefore, came to read quite a lot of Shakespeare in Swahili by Nyerere but remained relatively unaware of Mushi's

Swahili rendering of another of Shakespeare's plays. The other reason may have been the stature of Nyerere as a greatly admired pan-African leader and a relentless advocate of the Swahili language. But it is also possible that the choice of the two translations was inspired by thematic considerations.

Julius Caesar, for example, raised the important question of personality cult in the new nations of Africa and the possibility that the cult would develop a monarchical face. Nyerere himself was admired by Tanzanians and other Africans because of his modesty and his deliberate attempts to play down the personality factor in his leadership. "Indeed, Nyerere tried to discourage even such minimal ways of personal adulation as having streets named after him, or having too many photographs of himself distributed to the public" (Mazrui 1975, 116). In Tanzania, in other words, *Juliasi Kaizari* became relevant because of Nyerere's own style of leadership.

Across the border in Kenya, on the other hand, Jomo Kenyatta, the first president of the country, and Daniel Arap Moi, his successor, betrayed obvious monarchical tendencies arising directly from the personality cult they cultivated during their presidential tenure. Having streets, airports, or universities named after the presidents and their pictures displayed in all public places became unwritten laws of the country. Both presidents began to regard themselves as being above the laws of the country and as the personal embodiment of "the people" as well as the state. The theme of personality cult developing into a de facto monarchy that is inherent in Shakespeare's *Julius Caesar*, therefore, became an important mirror upon which Kenyan students could reflect, even if silently, on the leadership styles of both Jomo Kenyatta and Daniel Arap Moi.[2]

On the other hand, by the time Nyerere translated *The Merchant of Venice* into Swahili he was a declared advocate of *ujamaa*. The very term that Nyerere chose for his nation's brand of socialism—*ujamaa*—alludes to a certain bonding of kinship among the citizens and the quasi-familial obligations they had to share in order to help each other for the collective welfare of the society (instead of taking advantage of each others' misery). The themes of money as capital and of exploitation based on the unfortunate conditions of others that are part of Shakespeare's *The Merchant of Venice*, therefore, are likely to have been of direct relevance to the *ujamaa* experiment in Tanzania. It is very telling of the ideological motives of Nyerere, in fact, that he titled his translation *Mapebari wa Venisi* (the capitalists or bourgeoisie of Venice) rather than simply *Mfanyi-Biasha wa Vensi*, which would have been a closer rendering of *"The Merchant of Venice."* By pluralizing the title of the play, Nyerere probably sought to highlight his belief in the class basis of economic exploitation.

The successive Kenyan governments have been unwavering in their commitment to capitalism. Nonetheless, until recently, there was an oppositional voice, especially among academics, in favor of a socialist order. This contestation metamorphosed into different forms depending on the political conditions: It initially expressed itself within a single political party, the Kenya African National Union (KANU). It then became polarized into two contending political parties, KANU and the Kenya People's Union (KPU), and when the latter was banned, the socialist expression continued to operate underground until the 1990s, when the momentum for democratization changed the country's political landscape in a major way. So intense was the socialist pressure at one time that the government in power under Kenyatta was forced to produce a sessional paper entitled *African Socialism* that was intended to portray the mixed capitalist economy as a kind of socialism to give it a greater popular appeal. These political-economic conditions made the theme of capital raised in the *Merchant of Venice* of direct relevance to Kenya. It is quite significant that all the students' guides to the Swahili translation of *The Merchant of Venice* explicitly identify the conflict between capitalism and socialism as one of the themes of the play.

But if the counterideological thrust of the translations of these two Shakespearean plays was a core factor of their relevance in Kenya, how did they become selected for use in schools during a period when Kenya was in the throes of dictatorial leadership?

The circumstances were the same as the ones that led to the selection of the translation of Orwell's *Animal Farm*, to which discussion we shall now turn.

Orwell has said that *Animal Farm* "was the first book in which I tried, with the full consciousness of what I was doing, to fuse political purpose and artistic purpose into one whole" (quoted in Ingle 1993, 64). Politically, the work was intended to be a satire of the Russian revolution—its betrayal in the aftermath—to expose what Orwell called the "Soviet Myth," "the belief that Russia is a socialist country and that every act of its rulers must be excused, if not imitated." Artistically, Orwell thought of accomplishing this political mission "in a story that could easily be understood by almost everyone and which could easily be translated into other languages" (Orwell 1995, 179). And, indeed, the book quickly appeared in translation in several languages, including "Afrikaans, Danish, Dutch, Finnish, French, German, Greek, Icelandic, Indonesian, Italian, Maltese, Norwegian, Polish, Portuguese, Serbo-Croatian, Sinhalese, Czech, Slovene, Spanish, Swahili, Swedish, Ukrainian and Vietnamese" (Smyer 1988, 7).

The combination of both the formalistic elements and the political message were what initially drew the Swahili translator Kawegere to the novel. While the formal features of *Animal Farm* have been described as universal—traceable to Ovid, Aesop, Homer, and the Gospel of Mathew; the English classics of Dickens, Poe and Swift; and farther East to the Sanskrit *Panchatantra* and Buddhist *jakatas* (Smyer 1988, 9–10)—Kawegere regarded the animal fable as an enduring tradition of Africa and one that is particularly appealing to an African audience. According to Ruth Finnegan, the most familiar characters in indigenous African stories are animals, and they are often portrayed as thinking, feeling, and acting like human beings in human settings. A large proportion of this category of narratives consists of stories with a strong satirical tone (1970, 342–46).

In addition to the presumed inherent Africanity of the form used in *Animal Farm*, Kawegere attempted to domesticate the text further through a number of strategies. These have included what

Kenny has described as (a) normalization, seeking to make the translated text "conform to patterns and practices which are typical of the target language"; (b) lexical density, infusing the text with a higher "proportion of lexical as opposed to grammatical words"; and (c) sanitization, "the adaptation of a source text reality to make it more palatable to target audiences" (1998, 515–23).

Events in postcolonial Tanganyika—as mainland Tanzania was then known before its merger with Zanzibar—provided the immediate political context for Kawegere's decision to translate *Animal Farm*. As Venuti has rightly pointed out, the inscription of local target-community interests in the process of translation "begins with the very choice of a text for translation, always a very selective, densely motivated choice" (Venuti 2000, 468). In Kawegere's case, however, it was not the betrayal of the (anticolonial) revolution but the fear of an impending (socialist) revolution that became the inspirational force for his translation project. And this political motive of the translator betrays his ideological location both as a "strong" Christian and as a member of the Haya community, which was widely regarded as one of the more enterprising groups in Tanganyika. It was not an accident that the Swahili translation of *Animal Farm* was one among many translations of the text financed by the United States Information Service (personal communication with the translator), perhaps as part of the Cold War anticommunist offensive in the world.

It is true, of course, that the socialism of *ujamaa* was not formally launched, and the ruling Tanganyika African National Union (TANU) did not become the Chama cha Mapinduzi (Revolutionary Party) until 1967, the same year the Swahili translation of *Animal Farm* appeared. But the idea of a quasi-socialist state had certainly been in gestation as early as 1962—if not earlier—when Julius Nyerere, then the president of the country, released his pamphlet *Ujamaa: The Basis of African Socialism.*

Kawegere's fear of a socialist revolution in his native Tanganyika was further reinforced when the country merged with the independent state of Zanzibar to form the United Republic of Tanzania on April 26, 1964. This merger came barely three months after the Zanzibar Revolution, whose aims—given the role of the Marxist-led Umma Party as its engineer—were seen by many to be essentially communistic. It was even feared that Zanzibar would be an African Cuba of a sort—a fear that led to an alliance between Nyerere and the U.S. government that sought to nip the Zanzibar Revolution in the bud (Wilson 1989). To Kawegere, the Tanganyika-Zanzibar union was yet another clear signal that his country was gradually drifting to the left and that a Swahili translation of *Animal Farm* was urgently needed.

While Kawegere produced *Shamba la Wanyama* for his compatriots in socialist-leaning Tanzania, however, it was in capitalist Kenya, ironically, that the translation reached its greatest success. In 1994, the book was adopted by the Swahili Committee of the Kenya Institute of Education as an examinable text for the Swahili-literature paper for Kenya's high schools. Some of the most influential voices within this committee were left-leaning graduates of Nairobi and Kenyatta universities. These members of the Swahili Committee took the growing momentum for political reform in the country as an opportunity to widen the scope of the counterhegemonic discourse of the time by inscribing as oppositional the voice in Orwell's text that called for a more fundamental and systemic change in the political order.

The Kenyan revolutionary movement that can be compared most closely with that of *Animal Farm* is perhaps the Mau Mau movement against British colonial rule. Under the leadership of Dedan Kimathi, the Kenya Land and Freedom Army (KFLA) began the Mau Mau war in 1952. The colonial government's expropriation of much of the best land in the country for European settlers and a series of labor laws and regulations that forced Africans to provide poorly compensated labor for the settlers made land and labor the most burning issues in the struggle for independence. Under oppressive colonial conditions, Mau Mau became precisely the kind of revolutionary movement that partly inspired Orwell to write *Animal Farm*. It was a violent, conspiratorial revolution with a popular following. And while Mau Mau's military leaders may not have been known to be power hungry, those who claimed its political mantle and leadership and eventually assumed the reins of power when the country became independent in 1963 obviously were. It was a revolution that quickly opened the gates to its own betrayal, as Oginga Odinga, Kenya's first vice president, argued in his controversial book *Not Yet Uhuru* (1967).

A central theme of *Animal Farm* is the rewriting of history to distort the objectives of the revolution in general and the pig Snowball's role in the struggle for animal liberation in particular. This political exercise as it relates to the history of the Mau Mau came to be the hallmark of successive Kenyan regimes in the postcolonial era. Their silent policy has been "Speak no Mau Mau, hear no Mau Mau," which forced Kenyans to develop a culture of amnesia—to borrow Huyssen's phrase (1995)—about the movement and its leaders. As Ngugi writes, "The unavenged father's ghost of Kimathi's struggle and his KFLA walks the days and nights of today's neocolonial Kenya. The masses know it. So, too, do the ruling comprador bourgeoisie" (1986a, xvi). Ngugi posits that this is the reason for the continuing repression against those who seek to keep the historical memory of Mau Mau alive. On October 20, 2001, for example, over seventy Kenyans were arrested in the offices of the Release of Political Prisoners pressure group and charged with unlawful assembly. The group had apparently angered the government for declaring and celebrating October 20 not as Kenyatta Day—as officially named to mark the day of arrest of Jomo Kenyatta by the colonial government—but as Mau Mau Day in honor of Kenya's freedom fighters. Similarly, the Kimathi Cultural Center in Nyeri was denied permission to hold a celebration in honor of Dedan Kimathi on February 18, the day of his execution by the British colonial authorities. This was in 2006, when Kenya was seen to be at its most open politically (*Sunday Nation* [Nairobi], February 19, 2006).

The conduct of Kenyan leaders is also directly relevant. Under Jomo Kenyatta, the first president of the country, the mystification of the leader, the misappropriation of the products of people's labor, the kleptocracy and corruption in the highest circles of the government, the rabid authoritarianism of the regime, and the recurrent attempts of the regime to mislead the public on fundamental issues all bear a striking resemblance to some of the events in the life of the pig Napoleon in *Animal Farm*. And like Napoleon's political manipulations of Snowball in Orwell's tale, "communists" and critics of the government became scapegoats to cover up the regime's ineptness and mismanagement of the state. No wonder, then, that the Nyahururu Secondary School was immediately censured when it decided in 1976 to compete in the National School Drama Festival by staging a version of *Shamba la Wanyama*; the play was quickly banned.

Daniel Arap Moi, Kenya's second president, essentially followed in the footsteps of Kenyatta after his death in 1978. In the words of one member of Parliament, "Deterioration really set in [in] 1982, by which time there was no more freedom of debate for fear of falling foul of the party and the president. The days are gone when you could stand up in parliament and discuss what is in your mind—now it is considered subversion and treachery" (Africa Watch 1991, 17–18). Just as the general meetings in *Animal Farm* were progressively used to merely endorse the self-serving proposals of the pigs, so the Parliament in Kenya progressively became a mere rubber stamp for the wishes of the president and those closest to him.

Throughout the 1980s, fear of the "enemy" focused primarily on the universities that Moi's government monitored through informers. Many academics, students, and writers were forced into exile. In no time, Kenya had a huge population of political exiles, which was repeatedly accused of conniving with "imperialists" to undermine the popular will of the Kenyan people (as in the case of *Animal Farm*'s Snowball, who was accused of collaborating with Farmer Jones to destabilize Animal Farm). Those who remained and dared teach Marxist and other radical ideas were hounded out of the universities and imprisoned without charge or trial. Napoleon's dogs thus found their mirror image in the Special Branch police officers of Kenya, who often forced individuals to "confess" to crimes they had never committed.

In its attempts to combat "the enemy," Moi's regime strength-
ened its propaganda machinery. The government had always
owned the television and radio stations whose news broadcast always began with the day's engagements of "His Excellency."
Now it added a newspaper, *The Kenya Times*, to its media arse-
nal. Essentially playing the role of Squealer of *Animal Farm*, the
government-owned media became the most important organs for
justifying the unjustifiable actions of Moi and his government
and for covering up problems that faced the country, from
drought to famine, from the AIDS pandemic to the shortage of
medicines.

In due course, Moi developed a personal cult. No direct criticism was expressible in public, and the culture of fear and silence
that Jomo Kenyatta had managed to construct in the country
took even deeper root. In 1984, Moi declared, "I call on all ministers, assistant ministers, and everyone to sing after me like a par-
rot. You ought to sing the song I sing. If I put a full stop, you
should also put a full stop" (*The Weekly Review* [Nairobi], September 21, 1984, 4). Thus, the entire destiny of the country was
predicated upon how well its citizens parroted their president
and sang his praises. Moi rose above the party and the nation and
his voice became the voice of all. Daniel Arap Moi was now projected to be the epitome of human wisdom and above the laws of
the land.

Equally significant is the ethnocratic tendency of successive
Kenyan regimes—rooted in colonial history and founded in economic considerations—in which the president's ethnic compatriots and their "allies" are placed in a position of relative advantage
vis-à-vis members of other ethnic groups. Under Jomo Kenyatta,
it was the Gikuyu; under Moi, it was the Kalenjin. The privileging of the pigs of animal farm over other animals relates well to
this ethnocratic interpretation of Kenyan politics in the postcolonial period.

The dynamics of this ethnic politics during the presidency of
Daniel Arap Moi led to the production of yet another translation
of *Animal Farm*. This was a time when the Gikuyu people felt

particularly marginalized by a regime that was seen to be over-whelmingly dominated by politicians from the so-called KAMA-TUSA (an acronym for the ethnic alliance between Kalenjin, Maa-sai, Tugen, and Samburu). At one point, the Gikuyu were even described as the Igbo of Kenya, an allusion to their potential to foment secessionist ideas just as the Igbo of Nigeria are said to have done, actions that led to the eruption of the Biafra war. It was in this climate that W. W. Munyoro began to work on his Gikuyu translation of *Animal Farm* under the title *Mugunda wa Nyamu* (2002). From this ethnonationalist angle, the KAMA-TUSA oligarchy is compared to the pigs of *Animal Farm*—greedy, corrupt, tyrannical, and, above all, determined to downplay the role of the Gikuyu, the backbone of the Mau Mau movement, in the liberation of the country from European domination.

The contextual significance of *Animal Farm* in Kenya is by no means limited to the country's internal situation. It extends to Kenya's external relations. Some people have described Kenya as a neocolony: the local leadership is seen to be in collaboration with European and American big business to the detriment of the country's economy and the interests of the majority of its citi-zens. The dynamics of this state of neocolonialism is what Ngugi wa Thiong'o tries to capture in his *Devil on the Cross* (1980).

In his student guide to *Shamba la Wanyama*, Benedict Syambo specifically identifies *ukoloni mamboleo* (the Swahili term for neo-colonialism) as one of the main themes of *Animal Farm*. He suggests that there is little difference in terms of the suffering of the animals between what used to be the Manor Farm of Mr. Jones and what came to be the "Animal Farm" under Napoleon. And he points out that the colonialism that was brought to an end through the struggle of animals was reintroduced through the back door in a new guise (1995, 34–35). He draws a parallel here between Kenya's neocolonial condition and the trade relationship that de-veloped between Napoleon and humans to the exclusive advan-tage of the pigs of Animal Farm and the rich of the human world.

Even though *Animal Farm* was written to address the "so-cialist revolution" of the Soviet Union and was translated into

Swahili ostensibly to forewarn Tanzanians against an impending "socialist revolution," the reverberations of its political message were felt equally strongly in the staunchly capitalist nation of Kenya. And that message became the primary reason for the efforts of left-oriented Swahili educationists to use their influence, in the context of growing political opposition against the Moi regime, to inscribe *Shamba la Wanyama* as a counterdiscourse text in the Swahili-literature syllabus of the high schools of the country.

It is not only the "left" that sees particular advantages in the adoption of translated texts into the corpus of Swahili literary studies. There is some evidence that women in East Africa may have the same inclination. Sheila Ryanga, whose definition of Swahili literature includes translated texts, is of course, herself a woman—and in so defining Swahili translated text, she might have been inspired by the role they had in inscribing oppositional voices of women. For women, translated texts may function as potential instruments of counterhegemonic discourses against patriarchy.

This gender-based use of translation is amply demonstrated by an e-mail I received in January 2004 from Khadija Bachoo, an East African woman of Swahili-Muslim background. Bachoo was requesting from me a copy of an article that I had written on Nawal el-Saadawi's novel *God Dies by the Nile.* She wanted it as part of her background reading as she prepared to translate the novel into Swahili, motivated by the desire to communicate the novel's message to her Swahili community. She regarded *God Dies by the Nile* as a way of saying what she as a Swahili woman had wanted to say but was unable to do for reasons of cultural censorship. Because the translated work deals with a "foreign land" and a "foreign culture" out there, she believed it stood a better chance of escaping hostile reception from her patriarchal culture. Bachoo too, then, has favored the inclusion of (some?) translated texts in Swahili-literature courses to the extent that the linguistic movement of the text allows her to explore "the workings of gendered agency" (Spivak 2000, 397).

Coincidentally, Bachoo's sentiments capture quite well the irony of *God Dies by the Nile* as it relates to the Arabic original from which it was translated. Nawal had intended her Arabic original to bear a title that would actually translate into "God Dies by the Nile." But the novel finally appeared as *Mawt al-rajul al-wahid ala al-ardh* (The Death of the Only Man on Earth). The change was made at the insistence of her publishers in Lebanon, who regarded the Arabic title originally proposed by the author to be in violation of the religious sensibilities of Nawal's predominantly Muslim audience. In other words, if Bachoo felt that the translation of *God Dies by the Nile* from a foreign source to her native Swahili would give voice to women in her community, it is precisely the reverse phenomenon, the novel's translation from her native Arabic to a foreign one, that seems to have set Nawal's tongue free. In both cases, translation allowed the women writers to engage in a kind of social "unveiling" that, due to certain cultural rules of language use, original composition in their own native tongues would not readily admit.

The thematic relevance of translated works seems to have been one of the major factors behind the Swahili literary appropriation of Shakespeare and Orwell and perhaps of some other texts. *Mkaguzi Mkuu wa Serikali* (1979), the Swahili translation of Nikolai Gogol's *The Government Inspector*, provides an additional example. The theme of corruption the text raises, especially in the context of local administration (in the process enacting the conflicts between urban and rural), was of particular relevance to the Swahili-speaking regions of East Africa. Government overseers of *ujamaa* villages in Tanzania as well as mayors, district officers, and chiefs in Kenya became notorious for their record of coercive forms of corruption that were not dissimilar from those practiced by the mayor and his cronies in Gogol's novel.[3] This thematic focus of *Mkaguzi Mkuu wa Serikali* was one of the important factors that influenced its adoption in Kenya's Swahili-literature syllabus.

The teaching of translated texts as part of Swahili literature has not gone unchallenged. By all indications, however, those opposed to the integration of translated works into Swahili-language literature have been reacting more to the quality of translation than to the idea of a Swahili-translated literature (see Ryanga 1985, for example). The quality of Swahili translated works varies a great deal. A good many, unfortunately, are of rather poor quality even in purely Swahili linguistic terms.

Much of the rest of the discussion on translated works in Swahili, however, is unrelated to the definition of what we may call literature in Swahili. Rather, it has centered on the functions of translated texts in Swahiliphone Africa, which have included the following.

1. There is, first, the idea that translation is a way of exposing Swahiliphone Africa to experiences from other parts of the world and creating an avenue for cross-cultural understanding. For example, a significant number of English translations of literary works from nonwestern societies give English-speaking Europeans a glimpse of the "other." But a genuine cultural exchange, some have argued, must be based not only on making the "Third World" available to the Western reader but also on making the West available to the Third World.

What does get translated may not, of course, be free of certain ideological trappings and orientations. As a reflection of the relationship between the United States and many other nations in the post–World War II period, for example, "many foreign publishers . . . routinely translated large numbers of the most varied English-language books, exploiting the global drift toward American political and economic hegemony, actively supporting the international expansion of American culture by circulating it in their cultures" (Venuti 1992, 5). Aijaz Ahmad has argued that in translated works in the West in general, there is "a developing machinery of specifically literary translation" that has contributed to a false sense of a homogenous "Third World" literature (1992, 79), with all the political ramifications that such a construction implies. In this act of wholesale translation into English, Spivak adds, "there can be a betrayal of the democratic ideal into the law of the strongest. This happens when all the literature of the Third

World gets translated into a sort of with-it translatese, so that the literature by a woman in Palestine begins to resemble, in the feel of its prose, something by a man in Taiwan" (2002, 400).

After the 1967 Arusha Declaration in Tanzania, which launched the country on the *ujamaa* path, there was a noticeable increase of translated works with radical socialist-oriented content. These ranged from Frantz Fanon's *Wretched of the Earth* and Soviet texts on Marxist political economy to Maxim Gorky's *Mother* and children's stories from communist China. Fanon's *Wretched of the Earth*, in fact, appeared in two Swahili versions: *Mafukara wa Ulimwengu* (literally *The Destitutes of the Earth*, by Amhed Yusuf Abeid, published in 1977 by Transafrica of London) and *Viumbe Waliolaaniwa* (*The Damned*, by Gabriel Ruhumbika and Clement Maganga, published in 1978 by Tanzania Publishing House, Dar es Salaam). Ahmed Yusuf Abeid's Swahili rendering of the *Wretched of the Earth* was commissioned by the Tanzania Library Service Board. In the preface, the director of libraries mentioned several other Swahili translations that had appeared under their sponsorship, some focusing on specific pan-African leaders, including Julius Nyerere, Kwame Nkrumah, Patrice Lumumba, and Eduardo Mondlane.

And it is not only the production, circulation, and consumption of translated texts that may intersect with politics. Even what does or does not get classified as a work of translation may be politically determined sometimes. The racially purist politics of Nazi Germany, for example, led to the categorization of material that was originally written in the German language by Germans of Jewish origin as works of Hebrew in German translation in spite of the fact that the authors may not have known a word of Hebrew (Seyhan 2005, 286). Contrariwise, as I have demonstrated in this chapter in the East African context, certain translated texts can cease to be regarded as works of translation altogether for nationalist reasons of one kind or another. The ways in which politics and translation interact, then, are both multiple and varied.

Whatever their ideological orientation, the Swahili translation of works of European origin have been part and parcel of a dialogic process. The challenge that has confronted East Africans, especially in this era of post–Cold War globalization, is how to transform this process from a one-way infiltration of the Swahili literary space by the West into a two-way communication. Furthermore, how can the exchange be expanded to include not only the West but also Africa with itself and Africa with other parts of the world, such as India and China?

2. Translation has also been seen as a way of contributing to the transformation of "national literatures." Translation and creation have sometimes been regarded as interacting forces that lead to mutual enrichment. Octavio Paz, for example, has suggested that "there is constant interaction between the two [translation and creation], a continuous mutual enrichment. The greatest creative periods in western poetry . . . have been preceded or accompanied by intercrossing between poetic traditions. At times these intercrossings have taken the form of imitation, and at others they have taken the form of translation" (1992, 160). Translations, then, can sometimes lead to the generation of new forms and styles. They can serve as a catalyst for new developments in the literary tradition of a people. They certainly may have stimulated the emergence of both the novel and the play in Swahili literature, as they did the evolution of free verse.

When Nyerere translated Shakespeare using blank verse, he argued that he was using a "minority" verse tradition in Swahili called *guni*, which discarded rhyme. In his words:

> Mashairi ambayo hayana vina huitwa mashairi ya guni. Si mengi sana katika lugha ya Kiswahili lakini yapo. Nyimbo nyingi tuimbazo ni mashairi; lakini mengine huwa yana vina, na mengine hayana vina. Katika lugha nyingine vile vile mashairi huwa ya vina au ya guni. Katika kutafsiri *Julius Caesar* nimetumia sheria moja ya shairi la kawaida, yaani kila mstari nimejitahidi kuufanya uwe na mizani 16. Lakini mistari hii haina vina, wala haikugawanywa katika beti.

Poems that lack rhyme are called *guni* poems. These are not many in the Swahili language, but they do exist. Many of the songs we sing are poems, but some may have rhyme and others not. In other languages too, some poems may have rhyme and others may be *guni*. In translating *Julius Caesar* I have maintained one [prosodic] rule of ordinary [Swahili quatrain] poetry; that is, for every line I have endeavored to maintain a meter of 16. But these lines are without rhyme, and they are not divided into verses. (1963, 4; my translation)

In reality, *guni* is not a poetic tradition at all. The term usually refers to any poetic composition that is regarded as "faulty" either because it fails to meet, even if slightly, the prosodic rules of meter and/or rhyme. For all practical purposes, in using blank verse both Nyerere and Mushi were venturing into a mode of versification that was alien to the Swahili poetic universe of the time.

When Nyerere's translation of *Julius Caesar* was initially released, Ali Mazrui asked: "Did Julius Nyerere sacrifice some of the poetic power of *Julius Caesar* by retaining the blank nature of the original English verse? Should Nyerere have introduced rhyme into the play where Shakespeare himself had none?" In Mazrui's opinion, it was doubtful "whether readers of Swahili verse would enjoy blank verse at the same aesthetic depth as they now enjoy rhyme" (1967b, 127). To others such as Lyndon Harries, however, Nyerere's introduction of blank verse into Swahili literature heralded a new era, one in which Swahili poets would gradually free themselves from the 'fetters" of rhyme (*Sunday News* [Dar es Salaam], September 8, 1963).

Instead of inspiring Swahili poets to experiment with blank verse, however, Shakespeare's translation inspired them in the direction of free verse. If Nyerere's boldness dispensed with rhyme, a new generation of poets emerged that proceeded to dispense with both rhyme and meter of the traditional type. And in this innovative process a new poetic synthesis emerged in Swahili literature that fused old and new prosodic patterns into a distinctive creative product, with Nyerere's translation of Shakespeare as an important stimulus.

But the bias of translators toward texts of European origin poses the danger that the western influence on Swahili literature will be disproportionate. Because the East African region fell under British colonial rule, it is understandable that the linguistic competence of its academics would be virtually limited to translating between English and African languages. But even within this limit, there is a wide range of so-called postcolonial writing in English that has emerged in several countries outside the West. This literature has generally been ignored by Swahili translators. There have been translations of Voltaire, Shakespeare, and the four gospels in Swahili. But what about classical works from the Yoruba, Chinese, Judaic, or Hindu traditions? When will the Indian poet Tagore or the novelist Anita Desai be available in the Swahili language? The Qur'an already exists in Swahili, as do *The Thousand and One Nights*. But what about more recent classics of the culture of the Muslim world?

There was a time when Swahili literature drew inspiration and borrowings mainly from the Arab world. It now seems to have turned its attention exclusively to the literary experiences of the West. In this new orientation, however, is Swahili literature denying itself its full potential enrichment that can come only from the stimulus of more diverse civilizations? The answer may belong to the future as the Swahili literary canon continues to be reconfigured by the changing dynamics of East African societies.

3. In addition to enriching the literature, translations have also been seen as a way of validating and promoting the target languages. Nyerere may have viewed the prestige of Shakespeare as a literary aid in his own efforts to promote and consolidate the place of Swahili in his native Tanzania. According to Sheila Ryanga, the ability of Swahili to carry the literary experiences of other cultures belies the views of some scholars that Swahili is lexically poor. She has argued that

> utimilifu wa baadhi ya vitabu vya tafsiri na uthabiti wake unapinga maoni ya wasomi fulani wanaodai kwamba Kiswahili hakijitoshelezi kimsamiati kwa minajili ya kendeleza fikra ngeni.

> the cohesiveness and depth of some of the translated texts contradict the views of certain scholars that the Swahili language is

not adequately self-sufficient in its vocabulary to express concepts of foreign origin. (1985, 172; my translation)

In the introduction to the first edition of his translation of *Julius Caesar*, Nyerere also described his work as a clear demonstration of Swahili's lexical breadth; but he also acknowledged that it would be partly through translations that Swahili would gain even greater lexical space. In Nyerere's words,

> Nitafurahi sana ikiwa tafsiri hii itawasaidia wanafunzi wenzangu kuendelea kujifunza Kiswahili zaidi ili waweze kukisema na kukiandika kwa ufasaha zaidi. Kiswahili ni lugha tamu na pana sana. Lakini utamu na upana wake hauna budi utumiwe zaidi ndipo utakapoongezeka.

> I will be very happy if this translation will assist fellow students in advancing their Swahili studies so that they could speak and write it more proficiently. Swahili is a beautiful and rich language. But its richness and beauty can be augmented only if put to novel uses. (1963, 6; my translation)

Martin Luther's translation of the Bible posed a new challenge to the German language, just as the translation of Heidegger into French compelled the French language to undergo a modification that would allow for the narrativization of unfamiliar ideas (Legrand 2005, 30). Similarly, by putting Swahili's lexical reach to the test, by forcing it to carry the cultural world of an alien people, the first president of Tanzania hoped that conditions would be created for the further expansion of the language's lexical resources.

Some people have also embarked on translation of European classics as a way of validating not the Swahili language at large but particular dialects of it. A good example is Abedi Shepardson and Hassan Marshad's translation of Bertolt Brecht's *Good Woman of Setzuan* (translated as *Mtu Mzuri wa Setzuan*; i.e., The Good Person of Setzuan). The dialect referred to as Standard Swahili has sometimes been seen as a British colonial imposition that has marginalized the historically more literary dialects of

Swahili, such as Kimvita and Kiamu. Shepardson and Marshad felt that the literary achievements of Brecht, then, would help Kiamu and Kimvita reclaim their literary territory and former prestige. In the opinion of the translators:

> Lugha yetu wastwani isiwe ni ile twaloteguliwa na wakoloni bali iwe ile fasihi itumikayo pwani yetu—yalokuweko kwa muda wa makarne kadha wa kadha kabla ya Wazungu kuja kutufundisha hichi Kiswahili chao. Lafudhi hii tui*t*akayo ni ile yenye msingi wa Kimvita. . . . Tafsiri hii ya matezo yalotungwa na Bertolt Brecht ni moja ya kha*t*ua za kuimarisha lengo hili.

Our standard language ought not to be the one selected for us by colonialists; rather, it should be the literary language of our coastal region—which was in existence for several centuries before Europeans came to teach us this their Swahili. The Swahili we want is the one based on the Mvita dialect [of Mombasa]. . . . And this translation of Bertolt Brecht's play is one of the steps towards the realization of this goal. (1980, i–ii; my translation)

In Canada, translators have rendered canonical western dramatists such as Shakespeare and Brecht into Québécois French as a way of according the language greater cultural authority and challenging "its subordination to North American English and Parisian French" (Brisset 2000). Likewise, the Kimvita translation of Brecht was designed to reinforce a cultural identity in the service of a subnationalist agenda.

In general, the ability of the Swahili language to convey European classics has been seen as a tribute to the language's literary might. And the promotion of the language through these translations is ultimately a contribution to the promotion of its literature.

The role of translation in promoting the target languages and literatures is not, of course, a peculiarly Swahili phenomenon. Referring to the impact of biblical translations in Europe, for example, Lowry Nelson has argued that at every turn translators of the Bible had to make difficult choices reflecting accuracy, intelligibility, and idiomatic grace. Those choices over many centuries helped to fashion not only Medieval Latin as a living language, but as a vast array of vernaculars in Slavic, Germanic, Romance and other language groups. European literature was a continuous beneficiary of this enterprise. (1989, 19)

Accordingly, works translated into Swahili may well have been exercising their influence, silently perhaps, on the destiny of the language and its literature.

The early-twentieth-century Catalan translator Joseph Carner celebrated the translation of Shakespeare into Catalan for more or less the same reasons that led Nyerere to translate Shakespeare into Swahili. In Carner's words:

In order for Catalan to become abundant, complex, flexible, elegant, it is necessary that the masters of every country be honored with versions in our own language and, in gratitude, endow it with every quality of expression and differentiation that it needs. In order to make Catalan literature complete, essential, illustrious, our spirit must be enriched with every fundamental creation. (Quoted in Venuti 2005, 194)

For both Nyerere and Carner, in other words, translation of Shakespeare was part of a wider nationalist project.

This same nationalist agenda sometimes determines the discursive strategy used in the translation. Mushi's Swahili translation of Shakespeare, for example, seeks to be sensitive to the local culture and local nuances. The objective in such nationalist translations is sometimes to efface the fact of translation altogether, to create an illusion of transparency, making "the reader feel as if he or she were reading, not a translation, but the original" (Venuti 2005, 182)

I have tried to show in this chapter how translation can affect the development of the literature of a people, sometimes in unpredictable ways. This impact may result, in part, from the choices the subaltern makes to appropriate particular translated texts and put them to specific uses, which are often counterhegemonic. In the process, the translator can even make the conceptual boundaries of the literature of the translating language more permeable, if by doing so it can better allow the subaltern to "speak."

The Swahili experience has also demonstrated that translation can sometimes be conceived of as *transtextualization,* as a transfer of texts from one lingocultural universe to another. Transtextualization can be regarded as an aspect of the much wider phenomenon called *transculturation,* a term used "to describe how subordinated or marginal groups select and invent from materials transmitted to them by a dominant or metropolitan culture. While subjugated peoples cannot readily control what emanates from the dominant culture, they do determine to varying extents what they absorb into their own, and what they use it for" (Pratt 1992, 6). In its cultural and identitarian sense, then, transtextualization feeds on both the original and target sources in such a way that the translated text gets transformed and ultimately infused with a new, often domestic, identity. The process involves "active reconstitution of the foreign text mediated by the irreducible linguistic, discursive, and ideological differences of the target-language culture" (Venuti 1992, 10).

As transtextualization, translation exposes the tension between the authority of the original and the autonomy of the translated text. Transtextualization stresses "the dialectics of difference [that are] collateral with sameness[,] establishing the link between the translator and the actor—both live their own paradox[,] which is to be faithful in difference, saying the same thing yet saying fatally something else" (Vieira 1994, 65). In this sense, then, translation can be seen as creating a "double" that is simultaneously an affirmation and a denial of the original.

Mushi regarded his translation of Shakespeare's *Macbeth* as a work that was guided less by the imperative of fidelity to the original than by the principle of sensitivity to the Swahili lingocultural universe. Mushi's compatriot, Julius Nyerere, on the other hand, claims to have undertaken a revision of his translation of *Julius Caesar* partly because of certain "errors" he had supposedly committed in the first edition. In spite of himself, Nyerere seemed to regard translation as a search for some cross-cultural equivalence in meaning and seems to have presupposed the possibility of an "errorless" translation that is faithful to the original. But as contemporary Brazilian translator Nelson Ascher argues, a translation virtually does not exist; rather "it is exactly the area [of mistranslation] that is the proper dimension [of a translated text], that which gives it an identity and allows it to have its own History" (quoted in Vieira 1994, 65).

It has been argued that the universal appeal of Shakespeare's works makes them predisposed to multiple appropriations by other cultures and societies. This seems to have been Harold Bloom's position when he suggested that "there is a substance in Shakespeare's work that prevails and that has proved multicultural, so universally apprehended in all languages as to have established a pragmatic multiculturalism around the globe, one that already far surpasses our political fumblings towards such an idea" (1994, 62). Shakespeare, then, is seen to represent not a western or European-centered experience but a universal expression that, through translation, can be claimed by each and every one of us, across the boundaries of class, ethnicity, gender, race, or religion.

If the Swahili language has accommodated Shakespeare because of the universal appeal of his works, the ambit of that universalism must be expanded to include several other translated works that have appeared in Swahili-literature courses in high schools or universities in East Africa. These would include Chinua Achebe's *Hamkani si Shwari Tena* (No Longer at Ease), Ayi Kwei Armah's *Wema Hawajazaliwa* (*The Beautiful Ones Are Not Yet Born*), Wole Soyinka's *Masaibu ya Ndugu Jero* (*Trials of Brother Jero*), Nikolai Gogol's *Mkaguzi Mkuu wa Serikali* (*The Government Inspector*), and George Orwell's *Shamba la Wanyama* (*Animal Farm*). It is possible that all these works have a certain transcultural appeal that may have enhanced their absorption into Swahili literature.

When all is said and done, however, it is true that use of translation in a way that reconfigures the boundaries of Swahili literature has so far taken place exclusively within the corridors of the East African academy. The general tendency, however, has been to confuse "Swahili institutional academic culture" (of the nontraditional type) with the "culture of the Swahili-speaking peoples" more generally. This situation naturally raises the issue of the postcolonial intellectual within the African context.

Anthony Appiah once applied the term "comprador" to "postcolonial intellectuals" located in the West. He argued that

> postcoloniality is the condition of what we might ungenerously call a comprador intelligentsia—a relatively small, western style, western-trained group of writers and thinkers, who mediate the trade in cultural commodities of world capitalism at the periphery. In the West they are known through the Africa they offer; their compatriots know them through the Africa they have invented for the world, for each other, for Africa. (1991, 348)

This mediation is accomplished in part through writings in imperial languages such as English and in part through translation into imperial languages—all of which contribute to the imagining of an African canon within the western academy.

The condition described by Appiah can also be extended to the East African scene. For, bearing in mind that the African university still remains predominantly western in cultural terms, it is a tiny group of western-style, western-trained Swahilists who seek to make certain inscriptions in the Swahili literary landscape in a way that results in new boundary configurations. There is little evidence that this reconceptualization of Swahili literature emanating from the African academy has found its way to the wider Swahili-speaking society, whose members, in most instances, have limited or no knowledge of English in its spoken and written form. The bug of hybridization that is said to be a peculiar feature of the postcolonial condition may indeed be influencing Swahili literature toward increasing westernization. As academics in Anglophone Africa seek to Africanize writing in English, are African literatures in indigenous tongues as inscribed in the corridors of the postcolonial African academy themselves in danger of being de-Africanized?[4] The struggle continues.

Conclusion

The chapters in this book have tried to demonstrate how Swahili literature as a hybrid phenomenon from the earliest times has been undergoing (a new wave of) reconfiguration as a result of a conjuncture of new historical forces. While chapter 1 provided a general overview of the continuous reshaping of the Swahili literary experience (including the emergence of new literary genres), chapters 2, 3, and 4 focused on particular areas and themes within an indeterminate space of hybridization. In each of the latter three chapters, furthermore, we saw how socioeconomic factors in their colonial and postcolonial articulations led to new class formations, a development that is at the center of the contestation over the boundaries of Swahili literature. In spite of the efforts of a more "traditional" elite to restrict the frontiers of Swahili literature from moving in certain new directions, there is no doubt that a new literary syncretism is in the making.

As discussed in chapter 1 also, Swahili translation of European literary classics was partly intended to stimulate the development of the novelistic genre in Swahili literature. Yet, ironically, this tradition of translation later had a more direct impact on Swahili literary identity (as shown in chapter 4). The English classics that were translated during the colonial period and used as readers in schools retained an exclusively "foreign" identity in the Swahili literary imagination. This contrasts sharply with translations of Arabic classics such as the *Hamziyya* and *Alfu Lela Ulela* (*The Thousand and One Nights*). These became readily absorbed into the body of Swahli literature seemingly irrespective of the nationality of the translator. But when political conditions changed and Africans began to undertake the task of translation, some of the translations of English classics also came to acquire a new value and a new meaning in the world of Swahili literature. I have argued that the shortage of texts (especially plays and novels) on the eve of independence in East Africa may be part of the explanation for the Swahili literary appropriation of some translated materials. Now that Swahili creative texts are plentiful, will this change the entire literary relationship with translated texts? Will translated texts increasingly cease to be regarded as part of the corpus of Swahili literature?

Most Swahili translations from the Arabo-Islamic world undertaken by the Swahili have been in the form of verse. Most of the translations of English classics, on the other hand, have been plays and novels. When these get incorporated into Swahili literature, the motives are sometimes subversive. The translation comes to serve a counterhegemonic function in a political environment that allows only limited space for political criticism. The new millennium, however, has come with a more open political space in the region that allows free expression of political dissent. Texts critical of the state need no longer be hidden under the cover of foreign authorship and can be drawn directly from the pool of local literary material in Swahili without the fear of political repercussion. This new dynamic may also affect the extent to which translated works become Swahilized in literary identity.

An equally important area that framed twentieth-century debates on Swahili literary identity is the verse tradition—and more specifically its diction and poetic style and its thematic scope— pitting those who sought to maintain the "status quo" against new forces of poetic "modernization." Chapter 2 argues that the main reason poetry became such a contested space may have been that it is in this artistic terrain, especially in religious poetry, that the traditional Swahili intellectual elite was most intensely vested. The rise of new poetic forms outside the ambit of their creative genius challenged their class status within the Swahili-cum-intellectual tradition. And the marginalization of women in the Swahili circle of elite (which was defined mainly by literacy types and Islamic epistemology) marginalized women's voices in this debate.

This debate on Swahili poetry has invariably been expressed in terms of influences from the East (the Arabo-Islamic world especially) and the West, with nationalists of both camps claiming roots in an indigenous past. But it would be wrong to consider the indigenous legacy only in static terms of what used to exist at some point in history. The indigenous is also dynamic, evolving both from within as well as from interactions with other African communities with distinct artistic expressive cultures. Though internal migration has always been a feature of East African societies, it has picked up fresh momentum in the last couple of decades due mainly to economic reasons. This increasing internal migration in East Africa has been harmonious in some areas and periods and conflictual in others. How is this increasing interethnic interaction affecting the destiny of Swahili literature?

In 1997, there was a violent eruption on the coast of Kenya that was seemingly intended to "cleanse" the area of Kenyans of non-coastal origin. While by all indications the tragedy was politically orchestrated from the top, it fed on local sentiments that regarded "upcountry" Kenyans living on the coast as economic usurpers that were appropriating the best land, the best businesses, and the best jobs. The most militant of the coastal ethnonationalists were disenfranchised youth. Members of a social group from this class of the youth were once seen performing Alamin Mazrui's poem "Vitaturudia Tena" (Kenya Human Rights Commission 1998, 47):

> Kwa sisi wanao habibu
> Kwa wale wengi, wengi mno, wanaosulubu

Kwa wale wenye nyoyo zilizojaa ghadhabu
Na kwetu sisi warithi tulionyang'anywa
    tuloungana kama bawabu
Kwetu sisi sote . . .
Vyote vitakuja
Vitaturudia pamoja
Vitakuwa vyetu tena siku moja . . .

Kwa wale wanaoweza kungojea
Kwa wale wanaoweza kuvumilia
Kwa wale wenye majaraha, waloumia
Walothamini usiku wa baridi
    Uhuru kuupigania
Kuliko mwezi na nyota kuzifurahia
    Hali ni watumwa, watu kuwatumikia
Kwa hao wote. . . .
Vyote vitakuja
Vitawarudia pamoja
Vitakuwa vyao tena siku moja.

To us, your loving children
To those many, far too many, who toil
To those with hearts filled with anger
And to us, the dispossessed inheritors
    Bound together as hinges in a door
To us all
All shall return
Returning to us together
To be ours again someday. . . .

To those who can wait
To those who can endure
To those who have suffered injuries
Who valued nights in the cold
    Fighting for their freedom
To enjoying the specter of a moonlit and starlit sky

While remaining slaves, serving others
To all those
All shall return
Returning to them together
To be theirs again someday.

(Mazrui 1988, 23–25; my translation)

Here was a poem being performed by a group that would normally have performed verse in traditional rhyme and meter. But their struggle led them to draw on a poem composed in free verse. Cultural transformation need not always emerge from harmonious interaction between groups. It can sometimes emerge indirectly from situations of conflict.

Over time, the place of free verse in Swahili literature has been fully consolidated, even as some members of the Swahili ethnic community continue to shun this mode of versification. One of the factors that has helped lend cultural legitimacy to Swahili free verse has been the emergence of ethnic Swahili writers who compose in that genre. These include Said Ahmed Mohamed from Tanzania and Alamin Mazrui from Kenya. Both these writers have experimented with a wider latitude of rhyme and metric combinations that, although they diverge from the norm, would be acceptable within both the conservationist and the liberalist paradigms. What began as an ethnically defined debate (more or less) on the aesthetics of Swahili poetry—in which conservationists are predominantly (but not exclusively) of Swahili ethnicity and liberalists are predominantly (but not exclusively) non-Swahili—has metamorphosed into a transethnic expression.

It is not only local dynamics that have influenced the development of Swahili literature. There have also been some global forces at play. First is the American face that globalization has increasingly been assuming. As the only superpower in the post–Cold War period, the United States has naturally become central in this globalization process. The globalization of empire that the British attempted in the formal sense has been carried further by America in an informal way, to a point where "Americanization in its current form is a synonym for globalization, a synonym that recognizes that globalization is not a neutral process in which Washington and Dakar participate equally" (Readings 1996, 2). And Americanization is increasingly coming to imply the end of national culture, the many varied responses to it notwithstanding (3).

When the British wanted to influence the direction of Swahili literature, they began translating some of their own literary texts into Swahili. Are we now likely to witness a mushrooming of translation of American novels and plays—adding to the translation of Alex Haley's *Roots*—into Swahili under the new era of American empire? What is more likely to take place is American sponsorship of translation projects from any part of the world— just as the United States Information Service commissioned the translation of Orwell's *Animal Farm* into Swahili and several other languages of the world—if such projects are deemed to further the ends of the neoliberal agenda.

On the other hand, American fiction enjoys a growing popularity among East African youth. Danielle Steele, Sidney Sheldon, John Grisham, and Jackie Collins (among others) have captivated the imagination of children of the East African middle and upper classes in particular. Many East African youth are more informed about American writers than they are about East African writers. In addition, American television is a powerful cultural force. It is probably true that most East Africans still turn to BBC radio for their international news and entertainment. But when it comes to television, American CNN, soap operas, musical performances, and movies dominate the East African airwaves. At one time, the stories of the British character Sherlock Holmes (authored by Sir Arthur Conan Doyle) inspired Zanzibar author Mohamed Said Abdallah, to compose his own series of Swahili detective novels with Bwana Msa as the Swahili Sherlock Holmes. How will the new hold of American audiovisual popular culture influence future generations of Swahili writers? The situation continues to unfold.

In addition to the increasing dominance of America in global affairs, the end of the Cold War has also virtually eliminated the competition between capitalism and socialism within Africa, where socialism was often a by-product of nationalism. Post–Cold War globalization, however, has now compromised the sovereignty of the nation-state. As Bill Readings asserts:

> Under globalization the state does not disappear; it simply becomes more and more managerial, increasingly incapable of imposing its will as the *political* content of economic affairs. . . . This hollowing out of the state is a process that appears to the erstwhile national population as "depoliticization": the loss of belief in an alternative political truth that will authoritatively legitimate oppositional critique. (Readings 1996, 47)

The combined effect of these two trends of development in Africa is the decline of state nationalism and conflicting state-nationalist ideologies. The decline of nationalism has had linguistic consequences with obvious literary implications, especially in Tanzania.

Even though Tanzania is linguistically heterogeneous, it has a local lingua franca, Swahili, with a strong sentimental and instrumental value to a large section of the local population. The aftermath of British colonialism in the country saw the rise of the nationalism of self-reliance, *kujitegemea*, and the socialist ideology of *ujamaa*. The linguistic and literary expression of this socialist nationalism was in the form of Swahili, the common person's language of Tanzanian nationhood. Tanzania thus came to distinguish itself as the one former British African colony with a language policy that posed a genuine challenge to English as an imperial language.

The end of the Cold War and the increasing role of the World Bank and the International Monetary Fund have reduced the militancy of Tanzania's nationalism and deradicalized its socialism. In time, both *kujitegemea* and *ujamaa* as nationalist ideologies lost their appeal to the Tanzanian population, opening new spaces for the "rehabilitation" of the English language and literature in English. Globalization threatened the supremacy of Swahili in Tanzania. The very leader, Mwalimu Julius Nyerere, who was instrumental in the Swahilization of Tanzania desperately attempted to save English from annihilation in his country. As Nyerere was reported to have said:

> English is the Swahili of the world and for that reason must be taught and given the weight it deserves in our country. . . . It is wrong to leave English to die. . . . English will be the medium of instruction in secondary schools and institutions of higher education because if it is left as only a normal subject it may die. (Quoted in Roy-Campbell 2002, 100)

With this presidential endorsement, the demand for the language began to grow rapidly, especially in the urban school system.

The results of the above developments include not only the decline of creative works of the socialist imagination in Tanzania but also a growing exposure to literature in the English language from neighboring Kenya and other parts of the world. There was a time when students in Tanzanian universities were exposed to a good proportion of writers from the East, from the socialist world. Gradually the gaze has been turning toward the West. What will be the likely impact of these developments on Swahili literature in the twenty-first century? And what will be the implications for Swahili literary identity? The situation is still unfolding.

As indicated in chapter 4, the motives of translation sometimes betrayed nationalist agendas, as, for example, when intended to promote a national language (such as Kiswahili) or a national ideology (such as *ujamaa*). But if nationalist ideologies are on the decline in East Africa, how will the situation affect the place of translated works of European origin in Swahili literature?

On the other hand, it is precisely the effects of cultural globalization that seem to have triggered greater demand for Swahili translations of the Qur'an. Islam is one ideology that poses the greatest challenge to cultural westernization, and translations of the Qur'an have become important in Muslims' resolve to check what they regard as the excesses of the hegemonic "other." But what about patriarchal hegemony within the community of Muslims? All the Swahili translations of the Qur'an have been done by men in spite of the fact that in the last few years women have begun to emerge as *ulamaa* in their own right. Will these women scholars of Islam one day translate the Qur'an into Swahili from a nonpatriarchal point of view?

The effects of globalization in eroding national sovereignty have also been felt in East African universities. The university has continued to be the source of the most prolific production of literary works in Swahili. Leading Swahili writers—novelists such as Euphrase Kezilahabi, Said Ahmed Mohamed, and the late Katama Mkangi; playwrights such as Penina Mlama, Ebrahim Hussein, and the late Jay Kitsao; and poets such as Abdillatif Abdalla, M. M. Mulokozi, and Kithaka wa Mberia, to name but a few—have either been faculty members or students of the East African academy. Recent World Bank and International Monetary Fund conditionalities, however, have been leading to the corporatization of the university throughout East Africa. As an accompanying feature of globalization, this process has resulted in "the generalized imposition of the rule of cash-nexus in place of the notion of national identity as determinant of all aspects of investment in social life" (Readings 1996, 3). The (East African) university is increasingly becoming a different kind of institution, one that is no longer linked to the destiny of the nation-state by virtue of its role as producer, protector, and inculcator of national culture. Both faculty and students are expected to reorient themselves toward this new vision and mission of the academy. How will this new role of the university in East Africa affect the destiny of Swahili literature? Does it spell the end of nationalist and quasi-socialist literature for the moment?

But every thesis has an antithesis. The hegemonic homogenization of neoliberalism may trigger a variety of creative acts of resistance that may result in the revalidation of the local and/or the particular. The synthesis that may emerge from this contestation is a "glocal" one. As suggested in chapter 1, Said Ahmed Mohamed Khamis is of the opinion that the Swahili novel of the 1990s onward already shows signs of a stylistic and thematic transformation triggered directly by politico-economic conditions precipitated by globalization (2005, 91–108), a formation that may be a unique fusion of the "new" and the "old."

The decline of state nationalism, on the other hand, has created a space for the renewal of experiments of regional integration. The East African Community once collapsed partly because of the tensions precipitated by nationalist ideological differences. Ideological convergence in the post–Cold War era has rekindled the initiative. Of course, regional interaction in Africa has never fully depended on official sanctioning. The literature about Africa as a whole is replete with references to the artificiality of its colonial borders. And what makes these borders particularly artificial is neither the multiethnic societies they have created nor the "tribes" they have divided. It is rather the very concept of precise borders in Africa's "traditional" cultures that makes them artificial. This partly explains why those living near border areas find it difficult to respect these boundaries as they seek to respond to the pull of family and culture across the borders. The reality on the ground, then, is one where borders have often served less as walls that divide than as bridges that connect the people.

Nonetheless, the official sanctioning of regional integration has no doubt increased cross-border human traffic, both at the upper horizontal level of the elite and business class and the lower horizontal level of the average citizen. The end result of this demographic exchange is not only the continuing consolidation of Swahili as a regional language but also a growing cultural convergence in some of the core political values. Tanzanian writers are widely read in Kenya, just as Kenyan writers are read in Tanzania, all contributing not only to the evolution of a common literary Swahili but also to a shared literary aesthetics in the language. In the introduction, I referred to the words of Rainer Arnold to the effect that Swahili literature "represents no more the Swahili culture and society of the coast only. But it is part and parcel of the society and culture of the new nations of East Africa. From the scientific point of view it would be more effective to label this literature as East African literature in the Swahili language"(1972, 69). In the wake of the unprecedented cross-border cultural exchanges we are witnessing today, Arnold's definition of Swahili literature is receiving new historical vindication. This inter-African exchange, of course, is by no means limited to East Africa. It takes many forms and moves in many directions. Particularly significant in this regard is Article 4 of the 2000 Asmara Declaration on African Languages and Literatures: "Dialogue among African languages is essential: African languages must use the instrument of translation to advance communication among all people." After East Africa gained its independence from colonial rule, Heinemann (EA) Ltd. published a series of translated texts by African authors from English to Swahili, including Achebe's *No Longer at Ease* (*Hamkani si Shwari Tena*), Soyinka's *Trials of Brother Jero* (*Masaibu ya Ndugu Jero*), Armah's *The Beautiful Ones Are Not Yet Born* (*Wema Hawajazaliwa*), and many others. Unfortunately, this translation project gradually died out. The Asmara Declaration now promises to renew it, and Africa World Press in Trenton, New Jersey, has taken a particularly keen interest in the initiative. In chapter 4 we saw how translation contributed to the shaping of Swahili literature. If the Asmara Declaration were to inspire a new wave of translated works, how would it affect the future of Swahili literature and the core of its identity? It is certainly unlikely to remain unaffected.

The migration stimulated by new forces of globalization is also not limited to East African countries but extends to other countries of the Great Lake region. There are now many Swahili-speaking communities also scattered in the Middle East, Canada, and the United States. Some of these are engaged in explicit efforts to create a home away from home, to reconstruct a Swahili-based identity in their new locations. Muscat, Oman, for example, has now become as much the home of *taarabu* songs and music as Zanzibar and Mombasa in East Africa. Some of those who now constitute the new Swahili Diaspora are distinguished writers, such as Said Ahmed Mohamed and Abdillatif Abdalla in Germany. Their new location is undoubtedly influencing their compositions in new ways both in thematic and stylistic terms, and given their stature in the world of Swahili literature, their work may in turn influence new generations of Swahili writers.

Globalization as westernization/Americanization in the post–Cold War period has also helped trigger the resurgence of militant Islam. Throughout the Cold War period the West tried to woo the Muslim world because it was perceived to be staunchly anti-Communist. We now know, for example, that the origin of Usama bin Laden's Al Qaeda network lies, in part, in U.S. support of the *mujahideen* fighters against the Soviet invasion in Afghanistan (Chomsky 2001, 18–19). In the aftermath of the Cold War, the West has tried to demonize Islam after discovering that the religion can be a powerful inspirational force against westernization. But far from subduing this alternative cultural and ideological paradigm, western hostility against Islam only served to intensify militant responses of its followers across the globe. Chande (2000) gives a comprehensive outline of the various expressions of the face of this militant Islam in Kenya, Tanzania, and Uganda since the 1990s.

In East Africa, the Islamic responses to the western cultural baggage of globalization have included a linguistic dimension. In particular, there have been growing efforts among East African Muslims to learn the Arabic language as an affirmation of religious identity as well as for the purpose of gaining greater access to Islamic knowledge. In some instances there have been demands for Arabic in local academies as part of a wider struggle for religious rights. This dual phenomenon—the intensification of political Islam and the quest for Arabic language—have encouraged East African Muslims to take a greater interest in cultural developments in the Muslim world. From a 2004 pilot survey on the coast of Kenya, there is already some evidence that Swahili poetry is increasingly being called upon to perform the expression of a Swahili religious identity, with many composers using religious-based periodicals as outlets. The ecumenical configuration of Swahili poetry continues to unfold.

Religion is only one side of the politics of identity that has been given a fresh impetus by the forces of globalization. The other is ethnicity. There are now several studies that demonstrate how the momentum toward democracy in Africa since the early 1990s has been conditioned by both local dynamics and global developments. What is significant for our purposes is that this same wave of the politics of pluralism has given new expression to ethnonationalism. As Jan Nederveen Pieterse rightly observes,

> Ethnic politics may represent a deepening of democracy as mobilization of hitherto passive, alienated constituencies in reaction to regional uneven development or internal colonialism, for instance when indigenous peoples who have been passive in earlier rounds of nation-building, assert their rights. Ethnicization may also be a consequence of a shift to multiparty democracy; conversely it may be used and manipulated as a means to sabotage multiparty democracy as in Kenya recently. (1996, 26–27)

One important manifestation of the ethnicization of politics in East Africa is the development of the so-called vernacular media, both print and electronic. In Kenya in particular, the Gikuyu-language radio station Kameme FM has been particularly successful. But there are others, prompted by the same desire to inscribe ethnonationalist voices in the new, plural, and competitive political dispensation. It is in this context that the Pwani FM radio station was established in August 2001. Like the old program *Sauti ya Mvita* that operated during the colonial period, Pwani FM is intended to cater to the particular cultural tastes of the Swahili-speaking people of the coast. Its programs include *taarab* songs, poetry recitation, and fictional prose narratives. While Swahili literature as a whole is being nationalized throughout East Africa, Pwani FM seeks to feature a peculiarly coastal outlook on that literature, reminding us once again of the words of Giddens that globalization "invades local contexts of action but does not destroy them; on the contrary, new forms of local identity and self-expression, are causally bound up with globalizing processes" (Giddens 1991, 367–68). The tension between the local and the global continues its dialectical journey, with the "new forms of local identity and self-expression" constituting, in many cases, actual acts of resistance.

Globalization has sometimes been seen as a force that generates hybrid identities (e.g., by Lionnet 1996). But as we have seen from the experience of Swahili literature, the fact of hybridity is by no means new and predates any notions of the postcolonial and the postmodern. Transethnic and transracial social relations in East Africa have existed for centuries and have sometimes led to the adoption or even creation of new exogenous elements and to processes of pidginization and creolization. Post–Cold War globalization has made the hybridity of Swahili literature more complex and has extended its tentacles in new directions. As Swahili literature continues to be reshaped, we can expect its interplay with parameters of Swahili identity to be in constant flux, with old boundaries shattered and new borders drawn.

Notes

Introduction: Hybridity Reconfigured

1. For some recent excellent studies on the Swahili people and their cultures, see, for example, Middleton (1992), Allen (1993), Kusimba (1999), and Horton and Middleton (2000).

2. Describing the Swahili as a person of "mixed Negro and Arab descent," Captain Stigand proceeds to comment that

> the Swahili is a cheerful and happy-go-lucky as the African; fond of humor, intrigue and power as the Arab. Like the Arab, but to an even greater extent, he lives in two separate worlds, one of words and one of deeds. If you judge him by his sentiments, you find a man of noble aspirations, lofty ideals, intelligent thoughts, devout, kind, sympathetic and honorable. If you judge him by his actions, however, you find a man low, sordid, cunning, thieving, slanderous, callous and ignorant. . . .
>
> For the proper understanding of the savage African, one must not look at him as a human being, but as a rather superior kind of animal. Looked on from this point of view, many of his actions and ways of thought are intelligible where otherwise they are inexplicable. To judge the African side of the Swahili nature he must be looked at from this standpoint. (Stigand 1913, 130)

To Stigand, then, the Swahili is a good example of cultural schizophrenia, perpetually divided between his African and Arab sides.

3. As in the case of English in Africa, the development and spread of the Swahili language well beyond its ethnic "borders" has raised some serious questions about the essence of Swahili literature and its link with Swahili identity. Topan captured this quandary quite well when he asked:

Is Swahili literature written only by the Waswahili? If so, who is an Mswahili—itself a controversial question. Is Swahili literature that literature that deals with the Swahili or East African way of life? Or is Swahili literature written by East Africans? (1968, 161)

4. I define linguistic nationalism as that brand of nationalism that is concerned about the value of its own language, seeks to defend it against other languages, and encourages its use and enrichment as a symbol of the Self.

5. By implication, Philipson's definition includes any works produced in any part of Africa where Swahili is widely used as a first or additional language, including places such as Rwanda and Burundi. In Zaire, the fortunes of Swahili may have improved further since Kabila (the father) and later Kabila (the son) took the reigns of power in that country. Both Kabilas are very proficient in Swahili and have used the language to mobilize anti-Mobutu forces. It is too early to tell, however, how this political factor will eventually impact the development of Swahili literature in Zaire.

6. Before the language spread beyond its ethnic borders it was already differentiated into several "primary" dialects such as Kiamu, Kimvita, Kiunguja, and so forth. During the British colonial period, a "standard" variety, based on the dialect of Zanzibar, was imposed from above. As the language continued to spread it underwent additional differentiation, giving rise to new dialects, some national, some ethnic-marked, and some based on class factors (which are particularly evident in the slums of Nairobi).

Chapter 1: The Intercultural Heritage of Swahili Literature

1. It is a curious fact of history that the indigenized Swahili version of the Arabic script did not acquire an independent designation (as it did in Hausa, for example). To the present it is only known as "khati ya Kiarabu" (Arabic script). Part of the reason may lie in the possibility that its attempted reform and standardization by Sheikh Al-Amin bin Ali Mazrui was not accompanied by any nationalist ideology.

2. Swahili translations of these and other European-derived texts were part of a regular reading list for the Swahili subject in elementary schools in the native Swahili-speaking areas of East Africa well into the final years of British colonialism.

3. Ibrahim Noor Shariff believes that the book was not authored by James Mbotela at all. He argues that the book betrays a level of Swahili

proficiency that is far too low for Mbotela, who was virtually a native speaker of the language. Shariff concludes that the author or co-author of *Uhuru wa Watumwa* was most likely a European missionary as part of the colonial anti-Islamic campaign in the region and that Mbotela's name was appended to it to give it greater legitimacy among Africans (Shariff 1988, 17–19).

4. With regard to African literature in English, there was once a debate as to whether the African novel was of an entirely foreign origin or had indigenous antecedents that helped stimulate its evolution and development. Adrian Roscoe is one of the writers who contended that the novel in Africa is a literary import from the West, that it had no known history of existence from the African past (1971, 75). Chinweizu, Jemie, and Madubuike, on the other hand, while not rejecting the stimulus of the contact with the West, present an extended argument to demonstrate that Africa must have had its own antecedents to the novelistic genre, rooted in the oral tradition (1983, 31). Abdul Nanji (of Cornell University) has been carrying out his own research, indicating that a novelistic genre was in existence in Africa as early as Ancient Ethiopia and Middle Egypt (personal communication, March 23, 2006).

In the case of Swahili literature, however, it is widely accepted that the genre is entirely of foreign influence, though no doubt once introduced, it too assumed its own local identity from the very beginning. The kind of African nationalism observed with regard to defining the African novel in European languages has not been expressed with regard to defining the Swahili novel. The medium, the Swahili language, in the composition of this relatively new genre seems to have been sufficient to rehabilitate and absorb it fully and unambiguously into the body of Swahili literature.

5. In the wider circle of scholars of African literature, there have been attempts to locate modern African theatre to the indigenous precolonial experience. According to Mwenda Ntarangwi, "Dhana ya tamthilia imekuwapo tangu asili na jadi hata katika jamii zetu za kiafrika kabla ya athari za kimagharibi kupitia ukoloni, kwa vile palikuwepo sanaa mbali mbali za maonyesho ambazo humithiliwa na tamthilia" (The idea of a play has been in existence since antiquity even in African societies prior to any European influences resulting from colonialism, in that there were various kinds of performances that were dramatized; my translation; 2004, 54). Here Ntarangwi echoes Ngugi wa Thiong'o, who posits the existence of a precolonial Kenyan drama that "was part and parcel of the rhythm of daily and seasonal life of the community. It was an activity among other activities, often drawing its energy from

176 / *Notes to Pages 38-47*

those other activities. It was also entertainment in the sense of involved enjoyment; it was moral instruction; it was also a strict matter of life and death and communal survival" (Ngugi 1986b, 37). And that drama, according to Ngugi, often expressed itself in rites, ritual, and magic (1986b, 38).

One of the few Africans to take issues with this claim of an indigenous African theatre is the leading Swahili playwright and dramatist Ebrahim Hussein. In response to Ngugi, Hussein argues:

> It does not need emphasizing to say that one finds rites and rituals in the mosque [where many Swahili go for worship]. And both Muslims and Christians do not particularly relish to refer to these rites and these rituals as theatre as such. In this regard theatre art shows itself to be more selective than Ngugi presents it. It does not recognize every rite and ritual found in African tradition as theatre as such. The position held by Ngugi is analogous to that held by a number of African writers during the 60s. The writers asserted or assumed that there was theatre in Africa and that this theatre was in the course of time injured by colonialism. (Quoted in Ricard 2004, 163)

It is perhaps correct to say that Hussein's position represents the sentiments of many Swahili people who do not regard modern Swahili drama as indigenous in its origins. The Swahili, of course, had a tradition of dramatic interaction in some of their musical and dance performances, in harvest and religious ceremonies. The extent to which this tradition might have contributed to the shaping of Swahili dramaturgy, however, is yet to be fully studied.

6. Ricard is cautious, though, about the extent to which Hussein could be described as "individualist." In his words, "The question about the autonomy of artistic creation leads to that of the autonomy of the individual. Today, Ebrahim is alone: does that make him an individualist? I don't know. His Tanzanian critics are forever reproaching him for his *ubinafsi* (individualism). Does any writing exist which is not individual? How can the subject's experience not be borne by an original trajectory?" (Ricard 2000, x).

Chapter 2: Aesthetics of Swahili Verse

1. Until his death in 1978, Shihabuddin Chiraghdin was the most articulate advocate of "traditionalist" aesthetics in Swahili poetry, often

confronting arguments with counterarguments that border on Swahili ethnonationalism.

2. There is, of course, the demographic factor that over 60 percent of the native Arabic-speaking population in the world is located in Africa. More significantly from a linguistic point of view, however, is the evidence that traces the possible "origins of the Ancient Egyptian, Hebrew, Babylonian, Assyrian and Arabic languages back to a Central African homeland" (Faraclas 1995, 175).

3. The "standardized" version of the Swahili Arabic script that was proposed by Sheikh Al-Amin bin Ali Mazrui was never fully adopted by everyone in the community, with the result that different users sometimes selected different letters of the Arabic alphabet to represent the same Swahili sounds.

4. Most of the poems in this collection were composed when I was at Kamiti Maximum Prison in Kenya, detained without charge or trial under the Preservation of Public Security Act.

5. There was a time when the Sapir-Whorf hypothesis had completely fallen into disrepute. More recently, however, it has been rehabilitated by the work of cognitive linguists. Not only is Whorf no longer understood to have been an absolutist in his linguistic relativism, there is now a considerable body of literature that is believed to support his argument, for example, that linguistic patterns influence our patterns of attention and categorization in a culturally specific manner.

Chapter 3: Religion and the Boundaries of Swahili Literature

1. Julius Richter, a member of the Berlin Committee, "delivered a diatribe during the Kolonial Kongress in 1905 against the pernicious influence of Islam everywhere in Africa. Isolating East Africa as the scene of the worst danger, he envisaged a mosque alongside every coastman's hut, and took the official support for Swahili to be blatantly pro-Islamic" (Wright 1971, 113).

2. A substantial section of Christian missionaries—the so-called Livingstonians—were guided by the principle that spiritual communication with Africans was best achieved within the context of their "tribal" milieu and media. They insisted on using the native languages of the African groups they encountered in their proselytization and evangelical activities.

3. This popular association of Kimvita with Islam and Muslims among the native speakers of Swahili was readily confirmed by my study on language attitudes in Kenya (Mazrui 1981a).

Chapter 4: Translation and the (Re)Configuration
of the Swahili Literary Space

1. Making an explicit link between the vocational school in Zanzibar
and Booker T. Washington's Tuskegee experiment, Johnson added:

> Hivi sasa kule Amerika wapo maelfu ya watu weusi walio
> wakulima ambao wanaweza kupata mavuno zaidi kuliko walivy-
> oweza kupata wazee wao katika wao wanakumbuka deni wanalo-
> daiwa na Washington na Tuskegee. Ikiwa hatuwasaidii wana-
> funzi wetu kufanya vitu bora kuliko walivyokuwa wakifanya
> katika siku za nyuma tutakuwa hatutimizi kazi zetu vizuri.

At present in America there are thousands of Black farmers
whose agricultural yields surpass that of the entire life of their
parents, and some of them remember the debt they owe to
Washington and Tuskegee. If we do not assist our students to
produce better things than they used to in the past, we shall not
have adequately fulfilled our mission. (Quoted in Alidou 1998,
28; Alidou's translation)

2. Mazrui (1967b, 121–33) also made a connection between *Julius
Caesar* and the pattern of presidential assassinations that was emerging
in African politics.

3. With the 2006 revelations of massive corruption at the highest
level of Mwai Kibaki's government, especially in relation to the so-
called Goldenberg and Anglo-Leasing scandals, there is renewed interest in the Swahili translation of Gogol's *Government Inspector.*

4. This observation has also been made by Ali Mazrui. In his words:
"The publication of Julius Nyerere's Swahili translation of Shakespeare's *Julius Caesar* occurred close to the emergence of Kenya as an independent nation. No one realized at the time that Nyerere's translation
of the English bard would one day be taught as part of Swahili literature in Kenyan schools. Is this part of what Edward Said, the Palestin-
ian man of letters, has explored in his book, *Culture and Imperialism?* Is
the African self still at odds with his colonized other? (Mazrui 1995c).

Bibliography

Abdalla, Abdilatif. 1971. *Utenzi wa Adamu na Hawaa.* Nairobi: Oxford University Press.

———. 1973. *Sauti ya Dhiki.* Nairobi: Oxford University Press.

Abdalla, Mohamed Said. 1960. *Mzimu wa Watu wa Kale.* Dar es Salaam: East African Literature Bureau.

———. 1968. *Kisima cha Giningi.* London: Evans Brothers.

———. 1973. *Duniani Kuna Watu.* Dar es Salaam: East African Publishing House.

———. 1974. *Siri ya Sifuri.* Dar es Salaam: East African Publishing House.

Abdulaziz, Mohamed Hassan. 1979. *Muyaka: Nineteenth-Century Popular Poetry.* Nairobi: Kenya Literature Bureau.

Abedi, Ahmadi Shaykh K. A. 1967. *Uongofu wa Tafsiri ya Kurani Tukufu.* Zanzibar: n.p.

Abedi, K. Amri. 1954. *Sheria za Kutunga Mashairi na Diwani ya Amri.* Dar es Salaam: Eagle.

Abedi, Suleiman H. 1980. *Sikusikia la Mkuu.* Ndanda-Peramiho: Benedictine Publishers.

Akilimali Snow-White, K. H. A. 1962. *Diwani ya Akilimali.* Nairobi: Kenya Literature Bureau.

Abrams, M. H. 1993. "Preface to the Sixth Edition." In *The Norton Anthology of English Literature,* 6th ed., vol. 1. New York: Norton.

Africa Watch. 1991. *Kenya: Taking Liberties.* Washington, DC: Africa Watch.

Aga Khan Foundation. 1998. *Project Brief: Madrasa Pre-School Programme in East Africa.* Geneva, Switzerland: The Aga Khan Foundation.

Ahmad, Aijaz. 1992. *In Theory: Classes, Nations, Literatures.* New York: Verso.

Al-Barwani, Sheikh Ali Muhsin. 1995. *Tarjama ya Al-Muntakhab Katika Tafsiri ya Qur'an Tukufu.* Abu Dhabi: Zayed bin Sultan al-Nahayan Foundation.

Al-Buhry, Sheikh Hemed. 1955. *Utenzi wa Wadachi Kutamalaki Mrima*. Edited by J. W. T. Allen. Kampala: Beuchamp.

Al-Kindy, Sheik Said Moosa Mohamed. 1995. *Asili ya Uongofu Katika Uhakiki wa Materemsho na Ubainisho wa Tafsiri*. Muscat, Oman: Al-Nahda Press.

Alidou, Ousseina. 1998. "Booker T. Washington in Africa: Between Education and (Re)Colonization." In *A Thousand Flowers: Social Struggles against Structural Adjustment in African Universities*, edited by Silvia Federici, George Caffentzis, and Ousseina Alidou, 25–36. Trenton, NJ: Africa World Press.

———. 2005. *Engaging Modernity: Muslim Women and the Politics of Agency in Postcolonial Niger*. Madison: University of Wisconsin Press.

Alidou, Ousseina, and Alamin Mazrui. 1999. "The Language of Africa-Centered Knowledge in South Africa: Universalism, Relativism and Dependency." In *National Identity and Democracy in South Africa*, edited by Mai Palmberg, 101–18. Cape Town: Human Science Research Council.

Allen, J. de V. 1993. *Swahili Origins: Swahili Culture and the Shungwaya Phenomenon*. London: James Currey.

Amana, B. 1982. *Malenga wa Vumba*. Oxford: Oxford University Press.

Amidu, Assibi A. 1990. *Kimwondo: A Kiswahili Electoral Contest*. Wien: Beitrage Zur Afrikanistik.

Anthony, David H. III. 2002. "Islam in Dar es Salaam, Tanzania." *Studies in Contemporary Islam* 4, no 2: 23–47.

Appiah, Anthony. 1991. "Is the Post- in Postmodernism the Post- in Postcolonialism?" *Critical Inquiry* 17, no. 2: 336–57.

Arnold, Rainer. 1973. "Swahili Literature and Modern History: A Necessary Remark on Literary Criticism." *Kiswahili* 42, no. 2 and 43, no. 1: 68–73.

Ashcroft, B., G. Griffiths, and H. Tiffin. 2003. *Post-Colonial Studies: The Key Concepts*. London: Routledge.

Balisidya, N. 1975. *Shida*. Nairobi: Foundation Publishers.

Banjo, Ayo. 1983. "The Linguistic Factor in African Literature." *Ibadan Journal of Humanistic Studies* 3: 27–36.

Banzi, Alex. 1972. *Titi la Mkwe*. Dar es Salaam: Tanzania Publishing House.

———. 1977. *Zika Mwenyewe*. Dar es Salaam: Tanzania Publishing House.

———. 1980. *Tamaa Mbele na Hadithi Nyingine*. Ndanda-Peramiho: Benedictine Publishers.

———. 1982. *Nipe Nikupe na Hadithi Nyingine*. Ndanda-Peramiho: Benedictine Publishers.

Beckson, Karl, and Arthur Ganz. 1972. *A Reader's Guide to Literary Terms*. New York: Noonday.

Bertoncini, Elena Zubkova. 1989. *Outline of Swahili Literature: Prose Fiction and Drama*. Leiden: E. J. Brill.

Bhabha, Homi. 1994. *The Location of Culture*. London: Routledge.

Biersteker, Ann. 1996. *Kujibizana: Questions of Language and Power in Nineteenth- and Twentieth-Century Poetry in Kiswahili*. East Lansing: Michigan State University Press.

Biobaku, S. O. 1982. "Local Languages: The Depository of a People's Cultural Heritage." In *Nigerian Languages and Cultural Development*, edited by Bashir Ikara, 76–84. Lagos: National Language Center.

Bloom, Harold. 1994. *The Western Canon: The Books and the Schools of the Ages*. New York: Harcourt.

Bohannan, P. 1980. *African Outline*. Harmondsworth, UK: Penguin.

Brecht, Bertolt. 1980. *Mtu Mzuri wa Setzuan*. Translated by Abedi Shepardson and Hassan Marshad. Nairobi: Kenya Literature Bureau.

Burhani, Zainab W. 1997. *Mwisho wa Koja*. Nairobi: Longhorn.

———. 2001. *Mali ya Maskini*. Nairobi: Longhorn.

———. 2004. *Kipimo cha Mizani*. Nairobi: Longhorn.

Burling, Robbins. 1964. "Cognitive and Componential Analysis: God's Truth or Hocus-Pocus?" *American Anthropologist* 66: 20–28.

Chacha, Chacha Nyaigotti. 1982. *Mke Mwenza*. Nairobi: Heinemann.

———. 1986. *Marejeo*. Nairobi: Kenya Literature Bureau.

Chande, Abdin. 2000. "Radicalism and Reform in East Africa." In *The History of Islam in Africa*, edited by Nehemia Levtzion and Randall L. Pouwels. Athens: Ohio University Press.

Chimerah, Rocha. 1995. *Nyongo Mkalia Ini*. Nairobi: Jomo Kenyatta Foundation.

Chinweizu, Onwechekwa Jemie, and Ihechukwe Madubuike. 1980. *Toward the Decolonization of African Literature*. Enugu: Fourth Dimension.

———. 1983. *Toward the Decolonization of African Literature*. Washington, DC: Howard University Press.

Chiraghdin, Shihabuddin. 1971. "Utangulizi." In *Malenga wa Mvita*, by Ahmad Nasir, ii–viii. Nairobi: Oxford University Press.

———. 1973. "Utangulizi." In *Utenzi wa Fumo Liyongo*, by Mohamed Kijumwa, edited by Abdilatif Abdalla, 1–12. Dar es Salaam: Chuo cha Uchungizi wa Lugha ya Kiswahili (Institute of Swahili Research).

———. 1974. "Utangulizi." In *Sauti ya Dhiki*, by Abdilatif Abdalla, iii–xii. Nairobi: Oxford University Press.

———, ed. 1987. *Malenga wa Karne Moja*. Nairobi: Longman.

Chiume, M. W. K. 1969. *Dunia Ngumu*. Dar es Salaam: Tanzania Publishing House.

Chogo, Angelina. 1974. *Wala Mbivu*. Nairobi: East African Publishing House.

————. 1975. *Kortini Mtu Huyu*. Nairobi: Foundation Books.

Chomsky, Noam. 1986a. *Language and Mind*. New York: Harcourt.

————. 1986b. *Knowledge of Language: Its Nature, Origin and Use*. New York: Praeger.

————. 2001. *9-11*. New York: Seven Stories Press, 2001.

Church Missionary Society. 1969. *Nyimbo Standard*. Nairobi: CMS.

Cory, H. 1958. *Sikilizeni Mashairi*. Mwanza: Lake Printing Works.

Dashti, Ali. 1971. *In Search of Omar Khayyam*. New York: Columbia University Press.

Fair, Laura. 2001. *Pastimes and Politics: Culture, Community, and Identity in Post-Abolition Urban Zanzibar, 1890–1945*. Athens: Ohio University Press.

Faraclas, Nicholas. 1995. "They Came Before the Egyptians: Linguistic Evidence for the African Roots of Semitic Languages." In *Enduring Western Civilization: The Construction of the Concept of Western Civilization and Its "Other,"* edited by Silvia Federici, 175–96. Westport: Praeger.

Farsy, Sheikh Abdallah Saleh. 1954. *Upotofu wa Tafsiri ya Makadiani*. Zanzibar: Zanzibar Printers.

————. 1966. *Tafsiri ya Maulidi Barzanji*. Zanzibar: Mulla Karimjee Mulla Mohamedbhai and Sons.

————. 1969. *Qur'ani Takatifu*. Nairobi: Islamic Foundation.

Farsy, M. S. *Kurwa na Doto*. 1960. Nairobi: East African Literature Bureau.

Fiebach, Joachim. 1997. "Ebrahim Hussein's Dramaturgy: A Swahili Multiculturalist's Journey in Drama and Theatre." *Research in African Literatures* 28, no. 4: 19–37.

Finnegan, Ruth. 1970. *Oral Literature in Africa*. Nairobi: Oxford University Press.

Fuss, D. 1991. *Essentially Speaking: Feminism, Nature & Difference*. New York: Routledge.

Gerard, Albert S. 1981. *African Languages Literatures: An Introduction to the Literary History of Sub-Saharan Africa*. Washington, DC: Three Continents.

Giddens, Anthony. 1991. *Modernity and Self-Identity: Self and Society in the Late Modern Age*. Stanford, CA: Stanford University Press.

————. 1996. *The Consequences of Modernity*. Cambridge, UK: Polity Press.

Glassman, Jonathan. 1995. *Feasts and Riots: Revelry, Rebellion and Popular Consciousness on the Swahili Coast, 1856–1888*. New York: Heinemann, 1995.

Gogol, Nikolai. 1979. *Mkaguzi Mkuu wa Serikali*. Translated by Christon Mwakasaka. Nairobi: Heinemann Educational Books.

Graham, Billy. 1975. *Malaika: Mawakili wa Siri wa Mungu*. Nairobi: Evangel Publishing House.

Hadithi Ingereza. 1900. Zanzibar: Universities' Mission.

Harries, Lyndon. 1962. *Swahili Poetry*. Oxford: Clarendon Press.

————. 1970. "Translating Classical Literature into Swahili." *Swahili: Journal of the Institute of Swahili Research* 40, no. 1: 28–31.

Hichens, William. 1940. *Diwani ya Muyaka bin Haji Al-Ghassaniy*. Johannesburg: University of Witwatersrand.

————. 1972. *Al-Inkishafi: The Soul's Awakening*. Nairobi: Oxford University Press.

Hodgkin, Thomas. 1966. "The Islamic Literary Tradition in Ghana." In *Islam in Tropical Africa: Studies Presented and Discussed at the Fifth International African Seminar, Ahmadu Bello University, Zaria, January 1964*, edited by I. M. Lewis, 442–59. London: Oxford University Press.

Horton, Mark. 1987. "The Swahili Corridor." *Scientific American* 257: 86–93.

————, and John Middleton. 2000. *The Swahili: The Social Landscape of a Mercantile Society*. Oxford, UK: Blackwell Publishers.

Hussein, Ebrahim. 1969. *Kinjeketile*. Nairobi: East African Literature Bureau.

————. 1970. *Alikiona*. Dar es Salaam: East African Publishing House.

————. 1971a. *Mashetani*. Dar es Salaam: Oxford University Press.

————. 1971b. *Wakati Ukuta*. Nairobi: East African Publishing House.

————. 1976. *Ngao ya Jadi/Jogoo Kijijini*. Dar es Salaam: Oxford University Press.

————. 1980. *Arusi*. Nairobi: Oxford University Press.

————. 1988. *Kwenye Ukingo wa Thim*. Nairobi: Oxford University Press.

Huyssen, Andreas. 1995. *Twilight Memories: Marking Time in a Culture of Amnesia*. New York: Routledge.

Hyslop, Graham. 1957a. *Afadhali Mchawi*. Nairobi: East African Literature Bureau.

————. 1957b. *Mgeni Karibu*. Nairobi: East African Literature Bureau.

————. 1974. *Mchimba Kisima*. Nairobi: Nelson.

————. 1975. *Kulipa ni Matanga*. Nairobi: Nelson.

Ingle, Stephen. 1993. *George Orwell: A Political Life*. Manchester: Manchester University Press.

Irele, Abiola. 1981. *The African Experience in Literature and Ideology*. London: Heinemann.

Jahadhmy, Ali A. 1975. *Anthology of Swahili Poetry*, London: Heinemann.

Jamaliddin, Abdulkarim. 1957. "Utenzi wa Vita vya Maji Maji." Supplement to *Journal of the East African Swahili Committee* 27: 57–93.

Kahigi, K. K., and M. M. Mulokozi. 1976. *Malenga wa Bara.* Dar es Salaam: East African Literature Bureau.

Kahigi, K. K., and A. A. Ngerema. 1976. *Mwanzo wa Tufani.* Dar es Salaam: Tanzania Publishing House.

Kandoro, Saadan. 1978a. *Mashairi ya Saadani.* Dar es Salaam: Mwananchi.

————. 1978b. *Liwazo la Ujamaa.* Dar es Salaam: Tanzania Publishing House.

Kareithi, P. M. 1969. *Kaburi Bila Msalaba.* Nairobi: East African Publishing House.

————. 1975. *Majuto Mjukuu.* Nairobi: Gazelle.

Katalambulla, F. 1965. *Simu ya Kifo.* Nairobi: East African Literature Bureau.

————. 1975. *Buriani.* Nairobi: East African Literature Bureau.

————. 1976. *Lawalawa na Hadithi Nyingine.* Nairobi: East African Literature Bureau.

Kazungu, E. Kadenge. 1984. "Maendeleo ya Fasihi ya Kiswahili." Unpublished MS.

Kenny, D. 1998. "Creatures of Habit? What Translators Usually Do with Words." *The Corpus-Based Approach,* special issue, *Meta* 43, no. 4: 515–23.

Kenya Human Rights Commission. 1998. *Kayas Revisited: The Post-Election Balance Sheet.* Nairobi: The Kenya Human Right Commission.

Kezilahabi, Euphrase. 1971. *Rosa Mistika.* Dar es Salaam: East African Literature Bureau.

————. 1974a. *Kichwamaji.* Dar es Salaam: East African Publishing House.

————. 1974b. *Kichomi.* Nairobi: Heinemann.

————. 1975. *Dunia Uwanja wa Fujo.* Dar es Salaam: East African Literature Bureau.

————. 1979. *Gamba la Nyoka.* Arusha: Eastern Africa Publishers.

————. 1990a. *Nagona.* Dar es Salaam: Educational Publication Centre.

————. 1990b. *Mzingile.* Dar es Salaam: Educational Publication Centre.

Khamis, Said A. M. 2005. "Signs of New Features in the Swahili Novel." *Research in African Literatures* 36, no. 1: 91–108.

Khatib, M. S. 1975. *Utenzi wa Ukombozi wa Zanzibar.* Nairobi: Oxford University Press.

Kiango, S. D., and T. S. Y. Sengo. 1972. "Fasihi." *Mulika* 4: 11–17.

Kibao, Salim. 1975. *Matatu ya Thamani.* Nairobi: Heinemann.

Kiimbila, J. K. 1966. *Lila na Fila.* Dar es Salaam: Longman.

———. 1971. *Ubeberu Utashindwa*. Dar es Salaam: Taasisi ya Uchun-guzi wa Kiswahili.

———. 1972. *Visa nya Walimwengu*. Dar es Salaam: Longman.

Kijumwa, Mohamed. 1973. *Utenzi wa Fumo Liyongo*. Edited by Abdilatif Abdalla. Dar es Salaam: Institute of Kiswahili Research.

King'ala, Yusuf. 1984. *Majuto*. Nairobi: Oxford University Press.

King'ei, Geoffrey. 1992. "Language, Culture and Communication: The Role of Swahili Taarab Songs in Kenya." Ph.D. diss., Howard University.

Kitsao, Jay. 1981. *Tazama Mbele*. Nairobi: Heinemann.

———. 1983a. *Bibi Arusi*. Nairobi: Oxford University Press.

———. 1983b. *Malimwengu Ulimwenguni*. Nairobi: Oxford University Press.

Kitsao, Jay, and Zachariah Zani. 1975. *Mafarakano na Michezo Mingine*. Nairobi: Heinemann.

Knappert, Jan. 1979. *Four Centuries of Swahili Verse: A Literary History and Anthology*. London: Heinemann.

Komba, Serapius M. 1978. *Pete*. Dar es Salaam: Institute of Kiswahili Research.

Krapf, J. L. 1850. *Outline of the Elements of the Kiswahili Language with Special Reference to the Kinika Dialect*. Tubingen: Printed by Lud Fried Fues.

Kuria, Henry. 1957. *Nakupenda Lakini*. Nairobi: East African Literature Bureau.

Kusimba, Chaparukha M. 1999. *The Rise and Fall of Swahili States*. Walnut Creek, CA: AltaMira Press.

Legrand, Pierre. 2005. "Issues in the Translatability of Law." In *Nation, Language and the Ethics of Translations*, translated by Sandra Bermann and Michael Wood, 30–50. Princeton, NJ: Princeton University Press.

Lihamba, Amandina. 1980. *Hawala ya Fedha*. Dar es Salaam: Tanzania Publishing House.

Lionnet, Françoise. 1996. "*Logiques metisses:* Cultural Appropriation and Postcolonial Representations." In *Postcolonial Subjects: Francophone Women Writers*, edited by Mary Jean Green, Karen Gould, Micheline Rice-Maximin, Keith L. Walker, and Jack A. Yeager, 321–44. Minneapolis: University of Minnesota Press.

Liyongo Working Group. 2004. *Liyongo Songs: Poems Attributed to Fumo Liyongo*. Koln: Rudiger Koppe Verlag.

Liwenga, George. 1974. *Nyota ya Huzuni*. Dar es Salaam: Tanzania Publishing House.

Lodhi, Abdulaziz Y. 1974. "Language and Cultural Unity in Tanzania." *Kiswahili* 44, no. 2: 10–13.

Maduka, Chidi. 1980. "The Concept of the Igbo Novel." *Kiabara* 3, no. 2: 183–97.

Mayoka, J. M. 1986. *Mgogoro wa Ushairi na Diwani ya Mayoka.* Dar es Salaam: Tanzania Publishing House.

Mazrui, Alamin. 1981a. "Acceptability in a Planned Standard: The Case of Kiswahili in Kenya." PhD. diss., Stanford University.

——. 1981b. *Mwongozo wa Mui Huwa Mwema.* Nairobi: Longman Publishers.

——. 1981c. *Kilio cha Haki.* Nairobi: Longman Publishers.

——. 1988. *Chembe cha Moyo.* Nairobi: Heinemann.

——. 1999. *Political Culture of Language: Swahili, Society and the State.* 2nd ed. Binghamton, NY: The Institute of Global Cultural Studies, Binghamton University.

——. 2004. "Gender, Religion, and Language Performance: Between Swahili and English." Unpublished manuscript.

Mazrui, Alamin, and Ali A. Mazrui. 1998. *Swahili, State and Society: Political Economy of an African Language.* Oxford: James Currey.

Mazrui, Alamin, and Ibrahim Shariff. 1994. *The Swahili: Idiom and Identity of an African People.* Trenton, NJ: Africa World Press.

Mazrui, Sheikh Al-Amin bin Ali. "Arudhi ya Kiswahili." Unpublished manuscript (copy in possession of Prof. Ibrahim Shariff of Sultan Qaboos University, Oman).

Mazrui, Ali A. 1967a. "Abstract Verse and African Tradition." *Zuka* 1, no. 1: 13–22.

——. 1967b. *The Anglo-Saxon Commonwealth: Political Friction and Cultural Fusion.* Oxford: Pergamon, 1967.

——. 1972. *Cultural Engineering and Nation-Building in East Africa.* Evanston, IL: Northwestern University Press, 1972.

——. 1975. *The Political Sociology of the English Language.* The Hague: Mouton.

——. 1986. *The Africans: A Triple Heritage.* Boston: Little, Brown.

——. 1995a. "Islam in Sub-Saharan Africa." In *The Oxford Encyclopedia of the Modern Islamic World,* edited by John Esposito, 2:261–71. New York and Oxford: Oxford University Press.

——. 1995b. "English as an African Language: The Postcolonial Balance Sheet." Paper presented under the sponsorship of the Department of English, University of Hong Kong, March 25.

——. 1995c. "Why Is Our Literature so Stubbornly European?" *Sunday Nation* (Nairobi), August 20.

Mazrui, Sheikh Muhammad Kasim. 1976. *Utumwa Katika Uislamu na Dini Nyinginezo.* Nairobi: The Islamic Foundation.

Mbatiah, Mwenda. 1989. "Kiswahili Poetry: A Stylistic Revolution." *The Sunday Nation* (Nairobi), June 4.

———. 1995. "Why We Shouldn't Sing Praises to English Literature." *Sunday Nation* (Nairobi) June 25.

———. 2004. *Wimbo Mpya.* Nairobi: Jomo Kenyatta Foundation.

———, ed. 2000. *Mwandawazimu na Hadithi Nyingine.* Nairobi: Jomo Kenyatta Foundation.

Mbenna, I. C. 1972. *Kuchagua.* Dar es Salaam: Maarifa.

———. 1976. *Siuwezi Ujamaa.* Dar es Salaam: East African Publishing House.

Mbogo, Emmanel. 1996. *Vipuli vya Figo.* Nairobi: East African Educational Publishers.

Mbonde, J. P. 1974. *Bwana Mkubwa.* Nairobi: Transafrica.

Mbotela, James. 1934. *Uhuru wa Watumwa.* London: Sheldon.

Mhina, G. 1971. *Mtu ni Utu.* Dar es Salaam: Tanzania Publishing House.

Middleton, John. 1992. *The World of the Swahili: An African Mercantile Civilization.* New Haven, CT: Yale University Press.

Miehe, Gudrun, Katrin Bromber, Said A. M. Khamis, and Ralf Groberhode, eds. 2002. *Kala Shairi: German East Africa in Swahili Poems.* Koln: Rudiger Koppe Verlag.

Mkangi, Katama. 1975. *Ukiwa.* Nairobi: Oxford University Press.

———. 1984. *Mafuta.* Nairobi: Heinemann.

———. 1995. *Walenisi.* Nairobi: East African Educational Publishers.

Mkufya, W. E. 1999. *Ziraili na Zirani.* Dar es Salaam: Hekima.

Mlacha, S. A. K., and J. S. Madmulla. 1991. *Riwaya ya Kiswahili.* Dar es Salaam: Dar es Salaam University Press.

Mnyampala, Mathias. 1965. *Diwani ya Mnyampala.* Nairobi: Kenya Literature Bureau.

Mohamed, Mohamed Suleiman. 1972. *Kiu.* Dar es Salaam: East African Publishing House.

———. 1976. *Nyota ya Rehema.* Nairobi: Oxford University Press.

———. 1978. *Kicheko cha Ushindi.* Nairobi: Shungwaya.

Mohamed, Mwinyihatibu. 1980. *Malenga wa Mrima.* Dar es Salaam: Oxford University Press.

Mohamed, Said Ahmed. 1978. *Asali Chungu.* Nairobi: Shungwaya.

———. 1980a. *Dunia Mti Mkavu.* Nairobi: Longman.

———. 1980b. *Utengano.* Nairobi: Longman.

———. 1980c. *'Sikate Tamaa.* Nairobi: Longman.

———. 1984. *Kina cha Maisha.* Nairobi: Longman.

———. 1985. *Si Shetani si Wazimu.* Zanzibar: Zanzibar Publishers.

———. 1988a. *Kiza Katika Nuru.* Nairobi: Oxford University Press.

———. 1988b. *Pungwa.* Nairobi: Longman.

———. 1990. *Tata za Asumini.* Nairobi: Longman.

———. 1996. *Amezidi.* Nairobi: East African Educational Publishers.

———. 2001. *Babu Alipofufuka.* Nairobi: Jomo Kenyatta Foundation.

———. 2002a. *Sadiki Ukipenda na Hadithi Nyingine.* Nairobi: Jomo Kenyatta Foundation.

———. 2002b. *Jicho la Ndani.* Nairobi: Longhorn.

———. 2005a. *Mfuko Mtupu na Hadithi Nyingine.* Nairobi: Kenyatta Foundation.

———. 2005b. *Arusi ya Buldoza na Hadithi Nyingine.* Nairobi: Longhorn Publishers.

———. 2006. *Dunia Yao.* Nairobi: Longhorn Publishers.

Moi, Daniel Arap. 1986. *Kenya African Nationalism: Nyayo Philosophy and Principles.* Nairobi: Macmillan.

Msewa, O. B. N. 1977. *Kifo cha Ugenini.* Dar es Salaam: Tanzania Publishing House.

Mshamu, Mwana Kupona binti. 1972. *Utenzi wa Mwana Kupona.* Edited by Amina A. Sheikh and Ahmed S. Nabhany. Nairobi: Heinemann.

Msokile, Mbunda. 1981. *Nitakuja kwa Siri.* Dar es Salaam: Dar es Salaam University Press.

———. 1992. *Misingi ya Hadithi Fupi.* Dar es Salaam: Dar es Salaam University Press.

Mtendamema, G. 1978. *Utotole.* Dar es Salaam: Longman.

Mughniyya, Sheikh Muhammad Jawad. 2003. *Tafsit Al-Kashif.* Translated by Sheikh Hassan Ali Mwalupa. Dar es Salaam: Alitrah Foundation.

Mugo, Micere G. 1976. "Gerishon Ngugi, Peninah Muhando and Ebrahim Hussein: Plays in Swahili." *African Literature Today* 8: 17–29.

Muhando, Penina [Penina Mlama]. 1972. *Hatia.* Nairobi: East African Publishing House.

———. 1974. *Heshima Yangu.* Nairobi: East African Publishing House.

———. 1975. *Pambo.* Nairobi: Foundation Books.

———. 1982a. *Nguzo Mama.* Dar es Salaam: Dar es Salaam University Press.

———. 1982b. *Lina Ubani.* Dar es Salaam: East African Literature Bureau.

Mulokozi, Mugyabuso M. 1975. "Revolution and Reaction in Swahili Poetry." *Kiswahili* 45, no. 2: 45–65.

————. 1979. *Mukwawa wa Uhehe*. Nairobi: East African Publishing House.

Mulokozi, Mugyabuso M., and Kulikoyela K. Kahigi. 1976. *Malenga wa Bara*. Dar es Salaam: Dar es Salaam University Press.

————. 1979. *Kunga za Ushairi na Diwani Yetu*. Dar es Salaam: Tanzania Publishing House.

Munyoa, W. W. 2002. *Mugunda wa Nyama*. Nairobi: Sarakasi.

Musa, Sheikh Said. 1986. *Maisha ya Al-Imam Sheikh Abdalla Saleh Farsy Katika Ulimwengu wa Kiislamu*. Dar es Salaam: Lillaahi Islamic Publications.

Musau, Paul M. 2004. "Taarab Songs as a Reflection of the Changing Socio-Political Reality of the Swahili." In *Swahili Modernities: Culture, Politics, and Identity on the East Coast of Africa*, edited by Pat Caplan and Farouk Topan, 175–91. Trenton: Africa World Press.

Mushi, J. S. 1969. *Baada ya Dhiki Faraja*. Dar es Salaam: Tanzania Publishing House.

Mushi, S. S., trans. 1968. *Makbeth*, by William Shakespeare. Dar es Salaam: Tanzania Publishing House.

Muyaka (wa Mwinyi Haji). 1940. *Diwani ya Muyaka bin Haji Al-Ghassany*, edited by William Hichens. Johannesburg: Witwatersrand University Press.

Mwaduma, S. 1974. *Simbayavene*. London: University of London Press.

Mwanga, Zainab M. 1983. *Kiu ya Haki*. Morogoro: Spark International Consultants.

Mwangudza, J. A. 1986. *Thamani Yangu*. Nairobi: Oxford University Press.

Mwimali, Sheri C. 1995. "Is Kiswahili Study Inferior?" *Sunday Nation* (Nairobi), June 25.

Nabhany, Ahmed Sheikh. 1985. *Umbuji wa Kiwandeo*. Nairobi: East African Publishing House.

Nasir, Sayyid Abdalla bin Ali. *Al-Inkishafi*. Nairobi: East African Literature Bureau.

Nassir, Ahmed. 1971. *Malenga wa Mvita*. Nairobi: Oxford University Press.

Ndibalema, Charles. 1974. *Fimbo ya Ulimwengu*. Nairobi: Heinemann.

Nduguru, E. A. 1973. *Walowezi Hawana Siri*. Dar es Salaam: Tanzania Publishing House.

Nelson, Lowry Jr. 1989. "Literary Translation." *Translation Review* No. 29: 17–30.

Ngare, Peter. 1975. *Kikulacho ki Nguoni Mwako*. Nairobi: Kenya Literature Bureau.

Ng'ombo, Amina Hussein. 1982. *Heka Heka za Ulanguzi*. Ndanda-Peramiho: Benedictine Publishers.

Ngomoi, John. 1976. *Ndoto ya Ndaria*. Dar es Salaam: Tanzania Publishing House.

Ngugi wa Thiong'o. 1980. *Devil on the Cross*. London: Heinemann, 1980.

————. 1986a. "Foreword." In *Kenya's Freedom Struggle: The Dedan Kimathi Papers*, edited by Maina wa Kinyatti. London: Zed Press.

————. 1986b. *Decolonizing the Mind: The Politics of Language in African Literature*. London: James Currey, 1986.

Nguluma, J. R. 1980. *Chuki ya Kutawaliwa*. Dar es Salaam: Swala.

Njogu, Kimani. 1997a. *Mwongozo wa Amezidi*. Nairobi: Longhorn Kenya.

————. 1997b. *Uhakiki wa Riwaya za Visiwani Zanzibar*. Nairobi: Nairobi University Press.

————. 2004. *Reading Poetry as Dialogue*. Nairobi: Jomo Kenyatta Foundation.

Nngahyoma, Ngalimecha. 1975. *Kijiji Chetu*. Dar es Salaam: Tanzania Publishing House.

Ntarangwi, Mwenda. 2003. *Gender, Identity and Performance: Understanding Swahili Cultural Realities through Song*. Trenton, NJ: Africa World Press.

————. 2004. "Uhakiki wa Kazi za Kiswahili." Unpublished MS.

Nyerere, Julius, trans. 1963. *Julius Caezar*, by William Shakespeare. Nairobi: Oxford University Press.

————. 1969. *Juliasi Kaizari*, by William Shakespeare. Nairobi: Oxford University Press.

————. 1972. *Mabepari wa Venisi*, by William Shakespeare. Nairobi: Oxford University Press.

Odinga, Oginga. 1967. *Not Yet Uhuru*. London: Heinemann.

Ohly, Rajmund. 1985. "Literature in Swahili." In *Literatures in African Languages: Theoretical Issues and Sample Survey*, edited by B. W. Andrzejewski, S. Pilaszewicz, and W. Tyloch, 460–92. Cambridge: Cambridge University Press.

Omari, C. K. 1971. *Mwenda Kwao*. Dar es Salaam: Institute of Kiswahili Research.

————. 1973. *Barabara ya Tano*. Dar es Salaam: Tanzania Publishing House.

————. 1976. *Kuanguliwa kwa Kifaranga*. Nairobi: Heinemann.

Omolo, L. O. 1971. *Uhalifu Haulipi*. Nairobi: Longman.

Orwell, George. 1961. "Politics and the English Language." In *Collected Works of George Orwell*. London: Secker and Warburg.

————. 1967. *Shamba la Wanyama*. Translated by Fortunatus Kawegere. Dar es Salaam: East African Publishing House.

————. 1995. *Animal Farm: A Fairy Story.* New York: Harcourt Brace.

Osodo, Felix. 1979. *Hatari kwa Usalama.* Nairobi: Heinemann.

————. 1982. *Mama Mtakatifu.* Nairobi: Heinemann.

Paz, Octavio. 1992. "Translation: Literature and Letters." In *Theories of Translation,* edited by Rainer Schulte and John Biguenet, 152–62. Chicago: University of Chicago Press.

P'Bitek, Okot. 1973. *Africa's Cultural Revolution.* Nairobi: MacMillan.

Philipson, Robert. 1990. "Swahili Literature and Identity: The East African Debate." Unpublished MS.

Pieterse, Jan Nederveen. 1996. "Varieties of Ethnic Politics and Ethnicity Discourse." In *The Politics of Difference: Ethnic Premises in a World of Power,* edited by Edwin N. Wilmsen and Patrick McAllister, 25–44. Chicago: University of Chicago Press.

Pike, Charles. 1986. "History and Imagination: Swahili Literature and Resistance to German Language Imperialism in Tanzania, 1885–1910." *International Journal of African Historical Studies* 19, no. 2: 201–34.

Pratt, Mary Louise. 1992. *Imperial Eyes: Travel Writing and Transculturation.* London: Routledge.

Rajab, Hammie. 1982. *Miujiza ya Mlima Kolelo.* Dar es Salaam: Busara.

————. 1984. *Roho Mkononi.* Dar es Salaam: Busara.

Readings, Bill. 1996. *The University in Ruins.* Cambridge: Harvard University Press.

Ricard, Alain. 2000. *Ebrahim Hussein: Swahili Theatre and Individualism.* Dar es Salaam: Mkuki na Nyota Publishers.

————. 2004. *The Languages and Literatures of Africa.* Trenton: Africa World Press.

Robert, Shaaban. 1945. *Koja la Lugha.* Nairobi: Oxford University Press.

————. 1947. *Pambo la Lugha.* Johannesburg: Witwatersrand University Press.

————. 1951. *Kusadikika.* London: Nelson.

————. 1952. *Adili na Nduguze.* London: Macmillan.

————. 1953. *Kielelezo cha Insha.* Johannesburg: Witwatersrand University Press.

————. 1967a. *Utenzi wa Vita vya Uhuru.* London: Oxford University Press.

————. 1967b. *Kufikirika.* Nairobi: Oxford University Press.

————. 1968a. *Utubora Mkulima.* Nairobi: Nelson.

————. 1968b. *Siku ya Watenzi Wote.* Nairobi: Nelson.

Rollins, Jack D. 1983. *A History of Swahili Prose.* Leiden: E. J. Brill.

————. 1985. "Early 20th Century Swahili Prose Narrative Structure and Some Aspects of Swahili Ethnicity." In *Towards African Authenticity, Language and Literary Form,* edited by Eckhard Breitinger and Reinhard Sander, 49–68. Bayreuth: Bayreuth African Studies 2, Bayreuth University.

Roscoe, Adrian A. 1971. *Mother Is Gold: A Study in West African Literature.* Cambridge: Cambridge University Press.

Roy-Campbell, Zaline M. 2002. *Empowerment Through Language: The African Experience—Tanzania and Beyond.* Trenton: Africa World Press.

Ruhumbika, Gabriel. 1974. *Parapanda.* Dar es Salaam: East African Literature Bureau.

————. 1978. *Uwike Usiwike Kutakucha.* Dar es Salaam: Eastern Africa Publications.

Ruo, Kimani. 1989. "Revolution in Kiswahili Poetry." *Sunday Nation* (Nairobi), June 11.

Ryanga, Sheila C. W. A. 1985. "Vitabu vya Kutafsiriwa na Fasihi ya Kiswahili." *Ufahamu* 14, no. 3: 162–75.

Saavedra, Arturo Jose. Forthcoming. *Utenzi, War Poems, and the German Conquest of East Africa: Swahili Poetry as a Historical Source.* Trenton, NJ: Africa World Press.

Sapir, Edward. 1921. *Language: An Introduction to the Study of Speech.* New York: Harcourt.

————. 1929. "The Status of Linguistics as a Science." *Language* 5: 207–14.

Sehoza, Samuel. 1921. *Mwaka Katika Minyonyoro.* Dar es Salaam.

Seme, William B. 1973. *Njozi za Usiku.* Dar es Salaam: Longman.

Sengo, Tigiti wa. 1978. "Utangulizi." In *Ushahidi wa Mashairi ya Kiswahili,* by S. A. Kandoro, iv–ix. Dar es Salaam: Longman Publishers.

Senkoro, Fikeni E. M. 1978. *Mzalendo.* Nairobi: Shungwaya.

————. 1988. *Ushairi: Nadharia na Tahakiki.* Dar es Salaam: Dar es Salaam University Press.

Seyhan, Azade. 2005. "German Academic Exiles in Istanbul: Translation as the *Bildung* of the Other." In *Nation, Language and the Ethics of Translation,* edited by Sandra Berman and Michael Wood, 274–88. Princeton, NJ: Princeton University Press.

Shafi, Shafi Adam. 1978. *Kasri ya Mwinyi Fuadi.* Dar es Salaam: Tanzania Publishing House.

————. 1979. *Kuli.* Dar es Salaam: Tanzania Publishing House.

Shariff, Ibrahim Noor. 1988. *Tungo Zetu.* Trenton, NJ: Red Sea Press.

————. 1991a. "The Liyongo Conundrum: Reexamining the Historicity of the Swahilis' National Poet." *Research in African Literatures* 22, no. 2: 153–67.

————. 1991b. "Islam and Secularity in Swahili Literature." In *Faces of Islam in African Literature*, edited by Kenneth W. Harrow, 37–58. Portsmouth, NH: Heinemann; and London: James Currey.

Simbamwene, J. 1972. *Kwa Sababu ya Pesa*. Dar es Salaam: Longman.

————. 1978. *Kivumbi Uwanjani*. Dar es Salaam: Transafrica.

Smyer, Richard. 1988. *Animal Farm: Pastoralism and Politics*. Boston: Twayne Publishers.

Somba, John Ndetei. 1968. *Kuishi Kwingi ni Kuona Mengi*. Nairobi: East African Publishing House.

————. 1969. *Alipanda Upepo na Kuvuna Tufani*. Nairobi: Heinemann.

Spivak, Gayatri Chakravorky. 2000. "The Politics of Translation." In *The Translation Studies Reader*, edited by Lawrence Venuti, 397–416. London and New York: Routledge.

————. 2001. "Questioned on Translation: Adrift." *Public Culture* 13, no. 1: 13–22.

Steere, Edward. 1870. *A Handbook of the Swahili Language as Spoken at Zanzibar*. London: Sheldon Press, 1870.

Stigand, Captain C. H. 1913. *The Land of Zinj*. London: Frank Cass.

————. 1915. *Grammar of Dialectic Changes in the Kiswahili Language*. Cambridge.

Syambo, Benedict. 1995. *Mwongozo wa Shamba la Wanyama*. Nairobi: East African Educational Publishers.

Tolmacheva, Marina. 1978. "The Arabic Influence on Swahili Literature: A Historian's View." *Journal of African Studies* 5: 223–43.

Topan, Farouk. 1968. "An Approach to the Teaching of Swahili Literature." *Swahili* 32, no. 2: 16–26.

————. 1973. *Aliyeonja Pepo*. Dar es Salaam: Tanzania Publishing House.

————. 1974. "Modern Swahili Poetry." *Bulletin of the School of Oriental and African Studies* 37, no. 1: 175–87.

————. 1997. "Swahili." In *The Encyclopaedia of Islam*, new ed., edited by C. E. Bosworth, E. Van Donzel, W. P. Heinrichs, and G. Lecomte, 9:917–18. Leiden: Brill.

Tucker, Alfred R. 1911. *Eighteen Years in Uganda and East Africa*. London: Edward Arnold.

Ugula, P. 1969. *Ufunguo Wenye Hazina*. Nairobi: Evans Brothers.

Venuti, Lawrence. 1992. "Introduction." In *Rethinking Translation: Discourse, Subjectivity, Ideology*, edited by Lawrence Venuti, 1–17. London: Routledge.

————. 2000. "Translation, Community, Utopia." In *The Translation Studies Reader*, edited by Lawrence Venuti, 489–500. London and New York: Routledge.

————. 2005. "Local Contingencies: Translation and National Identities." In *Nation, Language and the Ethics of Translation*, edited by Sandra Bermann and Michael Wood, 177–202. Princeton, NJ: Princeton University Press.

Vieira, Elsa Ribeira Pires. 1994. "A Postmodern Translational Aesthetics in Brazil." In *Translation Studies Reader: An Interdiscipline*, edited by Mary Snell Hornby, Franz Pochhacker, and Klaus Kaindl, 65–72. Amsterdam: John Benjamins.

Wamitila, K. W. 1999. *Nguvu za Sala*. Nairobi: Longhorn.

————. 2002. *Bina-Adamu*. Nairobi: Phoenix Publishers.

————. 2005. *Tamthilia ya Maisha*. Nairobi: Vide-Muwa.

————, ed. 2004. *Mayai Waziri wa Maradhi na Hadithi Nyengine*. Nairobi: Focus Publishers.

Wanjala, Chris L. 1995. "Kiswahili: Our Varsities Must Do a Lot Better." *Sunday Nation* (Nairobi), June 11.

Whiteley, Wilfred. 1969. *Swahili: The Rise of a National Language*. London: Methuen.

Whorf, Benjamin Lee. 1949. "Language, Mind and Reality." In *Language, Thought and Reality: Selected Writings of Benjamin Lee Whorf*, edited by John B. Carroll, 246–70. Cambridge, Mass.: MIT Press.

Wilson, Amrit. 1989. *US Foreign Policy and Revolution: The Creation of Tanzania*. London: Pluto Press.

Woodsworth, Judith. 1994. "Translators and the Emergence of National Literatures." In *Translational Studies: An Interdiscipline*, edited by Mary Snell Hornby, Franz Pochhacker, and Klaus Kaindl, 55–64. Amsterdam: John Benjamins.

Wright, Marcia. 1971. *German Missions in Tanganyika: 1891–1941*. Oxford: Clarendon Press.

Yahya, A. S., and David Mulwa. 1983. *Buriani*. Nairobi: Oxford University Press.

Yahya, Saad A. 1973. *Pepeta*. London: University of London Press.

Young, Robert J. C. 1995. *Colonial Desire: Hybridity in Theory, Culture, and Race*. London: Routledge.

Yusuf, Hamza. 2005. "Foreword." In Shaykh Al-Amin Ali Mazrui, *The Content of Character: Ethical Sayings of the Prophet Muhammad*, edited by Hamza Yusuf, iii–vi. New York: Sandala.

Index

The letter *n* following a page number refers to a note on that page.